WITHDRAWN   KU-267-011

CM 11 002092
'2
,99
333.33 2209
Mun

Appraisal Essentials

Residential Report Writing and Case Studies

WITHDRAWN

Mark A. Munizzo

Lisa Virruso Musial

WITHDRAWN

Dearborn™
Real Estate Education

LEARNING AND INFORMATION
SERVICES
UNIVERSITY OF CUMBRIA

This publication is designed to provide accurate and authoritative information in regard to the subject matter covered. It is sold with the understanding that the publisher is not engaged in rendering legal, accounting, or other professional service. If legal advice or other expert assistance is required, the services of a competent professional should be sought.

President: Mehul Patel
Vice President of Product Development & Publishing: Evan M. Butterfield
Editorial Director: Kate DeVivo
Editorial Project Manager: Amanda Rahn
Director of Production: Daniel Frey
Senior Managing Editor, Production: Jack Kiburz
Creative Director: Lucy Jenkins
Production Artist: Virginia Byrne
Assistant Product Manager: Erica Smith

© 2008 by Dearborn Financial Publishing, Inc.®

Published by Dearborn™ Real Estate Education
30 South Wacker Drive
Chicago, Illinois 60606-7481
(312) 836-4400
www.dearbornRE.com

All rights reserved. The text of this publication, or any part thereof, may not be reproduced in any manner whatsoever without written permission from the publisher.

Printed in the United States of America
08   09   10   10   9   8   7   6   5   4   3   2   1

Library of Congress Cataloging-in-Publication Data
Munizzo, Mark A.
  Residential report writing and case studies / Mark A. Munizzo, Lisa Virruso Musial.
      p. cm.
  Includes index.
  ISBN-13: 978-1-4195-9257-7
  ISBN-10: 1-4195-9257-2
  1. Residential real estate—Valuation—United States. 2. Dwellings—Valuation—United States—Case studies. I. Virruso Musial, Lisa. II. Title.
  HD1389.5.U6M85 2007
  808'.066333—dc22
                          2007019220

CONTENTS

ABOUT THE AUTHORS

Mark A. Munizzo, IFAS, is a Certified General Real Estate Appraiser in Illinois and the president of The Equity Network, Frankfort, Illinois. The Equity Network is a real estate appraisal and consulting firm serving the Chicago market. In addition to holding a Bachelor of Business Administration degree from St. Norbert College in DePere, Wisconsin, Mr. Munizzo is currently completing his graduate studies in real estate appraising at the University of St. Thomas in Minneapolis, Minnesota. He currently serves on the education council for the Appraisal Foundation Sponsors and is a member of the examinations committee for the *Uniform Standards of Professional Appraisal Practice*. In addition, Mr. Munizzo is a national instructor with the National Association of Independent Fee Appraisers (NAIFA) and received its Instructor of the Year Award in 2002. Mr. Munizzo is also a certified *Uniform Standards of Professional Appraisal Practice* instructor with the Appraisal Foundation. Mr. Munizzo is coauthor of *Basic Appraisal Principles*, *Basic Appraisal Procedures*, *Residential Site Valuation and Cost Approach*, and *Statistics, Modeling, and Finance*, and has reviewed and consulted on several real estate texts, including *The Language of Real Estate Appraisal*, *Fundamentals of Real Estate Appraisal*, *Income Property Valuation*, and *Modern Real Estate Practice*.

Lisa Virruso Musial, IFAS, president of Musial Appraisal Company in Riverside, Illinois, received her Bachelor of Science degree in Quantitative Methods from the University of Illinois at Chicago. She is a Certified General Real Estate Appraiser in Illinois and a practicing commercial real estate appraiser in the Chicago market. Lisa is a national instructor with the National Association of Independent Fee Appraisers (NAIFA), having received its Instructor of the Year Award in 2004, as well as a certified *Uniform Standards of Professional Appraisal Practice* instructor with the Appraisal Foundation. Ms. Musial is coauthor of *Basic Appraisal Principles*, *Basic Appraisal Procedures*, *Residential Site Valuation and Cost Approach*, and *Statistics, Modeling, and Finance*, and has reviewed and is acknowledged in several real estate texts, including *Income Property Valuation* and *Fundamentals of Real Estate Appraisal*.

INTRODUCTION

Congratulations! You are about to raise your professional knowledge and understanding to a higher and more detailed level. Even if you are an experienced appraiser, some of this information will likely direct your thought toward what your appraisal practice should consist of in the future. In our minds, the subject matter in the following pages should be considered the heart and soul of real estate valuation practice. From this day forward virtually everything around you will begin to take on a new meaning as you continue to commit yourself to your professional development. We say this with certainty as we ourselves are practicing appraisers, national instructors, and authors of educational materials for appraisers. The profession itself encompasses many disciplines of valuation beyond real estate, and transcends such disciplines as economics, the construction trades, business, finance, law, governmental administration, statistics, mathematics, geography, geology, mapping, and information sciences, to name a few.

Most of the concepts, methods, processes, and techniques that appraisers use today are the direct the result of studies performed within the academic community and most often from some other related field of study, rather than from valuation. Only until recently, as the profession has begun to formally define certain issues, has there been a refinement of terms that can be cited as unique to the appraisal profession. We see this as a new beginning for the appraisal profession. We call for a serious working relationship with formal academicians to further elevate the valuation profession by advancing a more comprehensive and practical education curriculum. We believe our curriculum to be the starting point of such a relationship.

The material in this text is largely focused on report writing with consideration for the appraisal process and the process of scope of work, and how these processes are interrelated. This text is intended to educate you in the processes of reasoning and report writing, and to aid you in developing critical thinking skills in all real estate–related analysis.

You are responsible for understanding the material in this text and for pursuing a greater understanding and application of this information in the future as you incorporate these methods and techniques into your appraisal practice. However, a single course in real estate appraisal will not qualify you to be proficient in any subject matter discussed. Successful completion of an entire curriculum and application of actual experience determines the competency of all professionals.

You will find that every action you take as a professional appraiser has the potential to dramatically affect how every appraiser worldwide is perceived. This is an awesome responsibility and we hope that you are up to the task. With responsibility comes liability, and we are hoping that you act accordingly.

This text is designed to aid in this development. Each section is designed with learning objectives and key terms. Within each section are lessons that divide the section into subtopics that conclude with lesson review questions or exercises to reinforce the learning process. It is imperative that the student complete all lesson review and section questions as well as all in practice problems and note any questions, comments, or concerns that you might have for the instructor to clarify. The course learning objectives by section follows, and should be reviewed prior to reading the remaining text material.

We hope that you enjoy this process and we wish you success in your professional development.

The *Uniform Standards of Professional Appraisal Practice* are copyrighted and promulgated by The Appraisal Foundation. They are subject to ongoing critique and to additions and corrections. The portions of the *USPAP* appearing in this book are reprinted with the permission of The Appraisal Foundation.

LEARNING OBJECTIVES

Section 1: Reporting and Reasoning

By the end of this section, participants will be able to

- distinguish between developing and reporting in an assignment;
- identify the steps in the critical thought process;
- recognize the reporting standards of *USPAP*;
- understand the basis of the scientific method;
- define relevant information in the critical thought process;
- understand relevant characteristics in an assignment;
- identify the four steps involved with scope of work;
- understand the five functions of managing the assignment;
- discern between specific data, general data, primary data, and secondary data;
- define reconciliation;
- understand the difference between data and facts;
- recognize the definition of argumentation;
- recognize the definition of rhetoric;
- recognize the definition of logic;
- recognize the definition of dialectic;
- distinguish between formal and informal logic; and
- understand the important points of effective communication.

Section 2: Report Writing

By the end of this section, participants will be able to

- define effective communication;
- be familiar with the various levels of audience expertise;
- understand the significance of audience assessment;

- recognize how to assess an audience;
- understand the strategy for effective communication;
- understand basic grammar;
- recognize the eight parts of speech;
- distinguish between essay and composition; and
- understand the process of essay.

Section 3: Form Reporting

By the end of this section, participants will be able to

- be familiar with the Uniform Residential Appraisal Report (URAR);
- be familiar with the history of the URAR;
- be familiar with the required exhibits; and
- describe the use of the URAR.

SUGGESTED READING

Basic Appraisal Principles, Mark A. Munizzo and Lisa Virruso Musial, Dearborn Real Estate Education (2007)

Basic Appraisal Procedures, Mark A. Munizzo and Lisa Virruso Musial, Dearborn Real Estate Education (2007)

ACKNOWLEDGMENTS

The authors wish to thank those who participated in the preparation of *Residential Report Writing and Case Studies:*

Steven Stratakos

REPORTING AND REASONING

LEARNING OBJECTIVES

By the end of this section, participants will be able to

- distinguish between developing and reporting in an assignment;
- identify the steps in the critical thought process;
- recognize the reporting standards of *USPAP*;
- understand the basis of the scientific method;
- define relevant information in the critical thought process;
- understand relevant characteristics in an assignment;
- identify the four steps involved with scope of work;
- understand the five functions of managing the assignment;
- discern between specific data, general data, primary data, and secondary data;
- define reconciliation;
- understand the difference between data and facts;
- recognize the definition of argumentation;
- recognize the definition of rhetoric;
- recognize the definition of logic;
- recognize the definition of dialectic;

- distinguish between formal and informal logic; and

- understand the important points of effective communication.

KEY TERMS

argumentation

assent

burden of proof

claim

controversy

critical thinking

critical thought process

data

dialectic

development

effective
  communication

evidence

facts

general data

hypothesis

inference

issue

logic

managing the
  assignment

presumption

primary data

reasoning

reconciliation

relevant characteristics

relevant information

reporting

reporting standards

resolution

rhetoric

rhetorical thinking

scientific method

scope of work

secondary data

specific data

warrant

LESSON 1: The Appraisal Process and Reporting

THE APPRAISAL PROCESS

At this point in your educational development you have likely mastered the concept of the appraisal process. You will recall that the appraisal process is a two-part *scientific method* of *developing* and *reporting*. The focus of this course will be to concentrate on the second part of the two-part aspect of the process known as reporting. You will also remember that the appraisal process, like all scientific methods, begins with *problem identification* and concludes with *communicating the results*. Remember that the last step in the *development* aspect of the appraisal process is to *reconcile* to conclusions and that *communicating the results* is the reporting aspect of the two-step function of the appraisal process. This means that communicating or reporting the results of the assignment is the last step in the overall appraisal process. (See Figure 1.1.) **Development,** therefore, begins with problem identification and ends with reconciliation, while **reporting** is synonymous with communicating the results and is the final step of the process.

Reporting carries with it a specific standard of practice and, depending upon the assignment type, a different standard is used to govern the requirements placed on the appraisal professional. As an example, Standard 2 of the *Uniform Standards of Professional Appraisal Practice (USPAP)* dictates the requirements of reporting under a real property appraisal assignment. Likewise, Standards 3, 5, 6, 8, and 10 all address the reporting requirements for the various disciplines of appraisal review, appraisal consulting, mass appraisal, personal property, and business valuation assignments, respectively. These are known as the **reporting standards** (see the current edition of *USPAP*).

The Scientific Method

In scientific study, the **scientific method** is a process that begins with problem identification and hypothesis development, and then continues with data collection, verification, and analysis to reach a conclusion. A *hypothesis* has a slightly different meaning under the scientific method than typically understood. In common language, a hypothesis is an idea or proposition used to explain certain facts, or to provide the primary assumption of an argument. We will discus argumentation later in this section. In common language, a hypothesis is the basis of an argument or the main point of the argument, while the term has a more formal connotation in scientific analysis.

FIGURE 1.1
The Appraisal Process—Communicating the Results

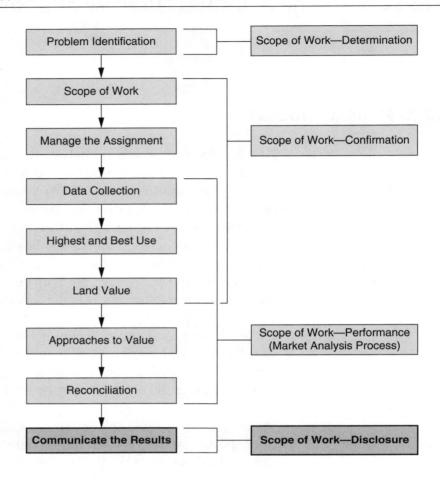

In the scientific method, a **hypothesis** is a formal statement that is carefully outlined and is the focus of a scientific inquiry that is to be tested based on the use of facts uncovered during the testing process. In scientific analysis, a hypothesis is a carefully crafted statement designed to be tested under the scientific method. As an example, Copernicus once set a hypothesis that "the earth revolved around the sun."

In most real estate analysis a hypothesis is not required. In fact, to set a hypothesis before data collection creates the risk of unduly directing the assignment toward either proving or disproving the hypothesis rather than allowing the market data to speak for itself. In such a case, the hypothesis becomes the focus rather than the market forces and factors that dictate answers to the identified problem. A hypothesis works well for investigations in the sciences, but it is the scientific method that is important to the real estate appraisal profession. Nonetheless, the scientific method is used without the use of a formal hypothesis as a means of conducting an appraisal assignment. As stated, the focus of this course is to concentrate on the final step of the appraisal process: to report the results of the development aspect of the appraisal assignment. While developing and reporting are two distinct aspects of the appraisal process, they are completely interrelated and should be conducted as such.

The purpose of setting an assignment to a standard based on the scientific method should be clear. The performance standards of any profession are strict requirements to ensure proper delivery of credible assignment results. By now it should also be understood that simply because the steps in the process are followed does not mean that the conclusions are foolproof. Critical thought plays an important role in reaching accurate conclusions. The appraisal professional must use his or her experience, specialized knowledge, and critical judgment to reach accurate and credible results during the execution of the assignment so that these results may be accurately communicated in the report.

As a means of reinforcing where the focus of this course will be placed, let us review the following detailed description of each step in the appraisal process.

Problem Identification

The professional appraiser must first identify the primary issues during the engagement process and determine from the start whether he or she has the experience and the knowledge to complete the assignment in a competent manner. This is known as the competency requirement for all real estate appraisers. The appraiser must determine whether the results of the assignment will be credible in light of the clients' intended use of the report. Simply because the appraiser has the education to conduct an assignment or may have completed similar assignments in other regions does not necessarily mean that the appraiser has the competency to perform this particular assignment in this area. The competency provision pertains to property types, geographical area, appropriate application of a recognized method or technique, and virtually any other experience or related issue that the appraiser might face. (See the Competency Rule in *USPAP*.)

The information that is required in the problem identification stage is known as **relevant characteristics.** Under the *Uniform Standards of Professional Appraisal Practice* an appraiser must "identify all characteristics of the property that are relevant to the type and value and intended users of the appraisal." (See Standard 1-2(e) of *USPAP*.) In the market analysis process, relevant characteristics are also required within the first step. This is to aid the appraiser/analyst in conducting data collection that is relevant to the assignment and, in particular, relevant to the subject property and use of the analysis.

Within this first step in the appraisal process, the appraiser must identify the following:

- The client and other intended users of the report

- The intended use of the report and the appraiser's opinions and conclusions

- The type and definition of value and the source of the definition

- The effective date of the appraiser's opinion and conclusions

- The description and location of the real estate

- The property rights to be valued

- The characteristics that are relevant to the type of value and the intended use of the appraisal, along with the limiting conditions or limitations of the appraisal (determine the scope of work)

Scope of Work

In addition to determining competency during the problem identification step, scope of work is also determined by the appraiser largely during the engagement process and interview with the client. Like competency, the appraiser must maintain the appropriate scope of work throughout the appraisal process. **Scope of work** determination begins with the engagement process and is confirmed once the property is inspected, data is collected and verified, and, in the case of a real property appraisal assignment, highest and best use is completed and the land value is concluded. Scope of work performance takes place from data collection and verification all the way through to reconciliation. Once all opinions and conclusions are completed, the scope of work is disclosed in the reporting or communicating process of the assignment. Therefore, there are four overlapping steps in the scope of work process that help ensure proper conduct within scope of work and market analysis:

1. **Determine** the proper scope of work, a preliminary determination

2. **Confirm** the scope of work, a confirmed determination

3. **Perform** the scope of work necessary, execute the scope of work

4. **Disclose** the scope of work in the report

The scope of work decision is largely dictated by the clients needs and intended use of the appraisal, along with the assignment conditions. The assignment conditions are those that may have an effect on how the information is analyzed and reported. Such conditions include situations where the appraiser is forced to make reasonable assumptions that are not absolutely known in order to complete the assignment. Assignment conditions must not affect the credibility of the assignment results.

Scope of work can be affected by circumstances in the appraisal, the property itself, or highest and best use analysis. There may be a change in how the appraiser will value the property if any of these circumstances are found to have shifted during the data collection stages. Scope of work is integrated in the appraisal process, and the process of confirming the scope of work and performing the scope of work are overlapped. (See Figure 1.1.)

Managing the Assignment

While it may seem that **managing the assignment** is separate from scope of work within the outline of the appraisal process, they are in fact concurrent processes. Once the engagement process is complete, the professional appraiser should have a clear understanding of the clients' needs and expectations. To enhance performance, the appraiser must manage the assignment. The five basic functions of management are as follows:

- **Plan**—To determine what is required, and when

- **Organize**—To determine how the assignment process will be conducted

- **Staff**—To determine the personnel required for the assignment and to identify that the competency of every individual associated with the assignment is appropriate

- **Direct**—To be certain that the relevant characteristics are identified and that the scope of work is appropriate throughout the assignment. It is also important to direct other associates working on the assignment, particularly if they are a trainee or an underling.

- **Control**—To ensure that the appraisal process is completed with accurate and verified information

A good management function also includes a feedback mechanism for oversight and for periodically calibrating the manner in which assignments are completed. *Feedback* is perhaps the most important safeguard against proceeding on an assignment in a perfunctory or robotic manner.

Data Collection and Verification

During the data collection and verification stage, the appraiser determines what information is most relevant to the analysis and how this information is related to the definition of the problem to be solved. Further, the quality and durability of the data uncovered during this stage is the basis for the opinions and conclusions that will be completed during the reconciliation stage. Much of the data uncovered will be applied during the various approaches to value, where a clearer interpretation of the data is more formally considered.

There are different types of **data** uncovered during an appraisal assignment. **Specific data** is data that relates directly to the subject property, and much of this information is collected during the inspection of the subject property itself. Typically, specific data is obtained as **primary data** or data that is uncovered firsthand by the appraiser. **General data** is data that relates to the neighborhood or region. Such information is typically obtained as **secondary data** or data that is received from a secondary source such as public records or census information. In truth, specific data and general data can be obtained as either primary or secondary data.

Data collection and verification is often where even the most experienced appraisal professionals fail to correctly employ due diligence. Gathering information is one thing, critically thinking about the relevance and accuracy of the information is quite another. Too often an unacceptable appraisal report contains excessive market-derived information that is not presented to the reader in a relevant manner. In short, data collection without analysis is a major omission and a pitfall for appraisers because such actions fell below the standard of practice.

Highest and Best Use

The first natural assumption that an appraiser must make is that the property will be properly managed and be put to its highest and best use. Within this use consideration rests the concern that an owner of a given property will seek out the most reasonably probable, physically possible, legally permissible, financially feasible, and maximally productive use of the property. These criteria are based on the market data uncovered and on the physical structure of the subject property.

Approaches to Value

Appraisers are taught early on that there are three traditional approaches to value in the appraisal process that the appraiser should complete if at all possible: the income approach, the cost approach, and the sales comparison approach. Each approach views problem identification from a different perspective. While each approach requires different data to be collected specifically for that approach to value, some of the data that is uncovered is used within each approach in a different manner. There are times when one approach may be more appropriate to value a property than another, particularly if the approach is more indicative of what is taking place in the market. Conversely, an approach may not be at all appropriate because of a lack of data or because the results may be potentially misleading or inaccurate, whereby the appraisal results lack credibility. Sometimes the approach may not be appropriate because of the property itself. As an example, the cost approach is not applicable in the case of vacant land as there are no improvements to cost. An indicated value conclusion within each approach is *reconciled* after determining the strengths and weaknesses of the data found and analyzed within each approach to value.

Many appraisers believe that the approaches to value are the most critical aspect of an appraisal assignment, and yet these are only tools of valuation, not necessarily the most thought-provoking part of the process. These tools of the assignment help the appraiser to reach conclusions that are uncovered during the market analysis section of the appraisal process. Once trends are identified during data collection and analysis, and value conclusions are indicated after the approaches to value are completed, overall conclusions can be made based on the information uncovered throughout the process. Such overall opinions and conclusions are *reconciled* from the approaches to value based on validity and quality of the information within each approach.

Reconciliation

During the reconciliation phase of the appraisal process the opinions and conclusions are sorted out in a comprehensive manner. **Reconciliation** is the process of determining and giving weight to the most relevant information to support the conclusions that are an accurate interpretation of the trends relevant to the definition of the valuation problem in the assignment. Reconciliation is performed at the end of each approach to value whereby the appraiser concludes an indication of value using that specific valuation approach. After the appraiser determines the value under each approach, the appraiser further reconciles to a final value conclusion. This *final reconciliation* is the process of giving the most weight to a particular approach over another based on which is most relevant to the problem in order to conclude a final valuation decision.

Another part of reconciliation that is commonly overlooked is the point that market trends and other such information uncovered within the market analysis are supposed to be included in these conclusions. Including this information helps to support or reject notions, either preconceived or concluded. These omissions are the result of an appraiser's unwillingness to use the critical thought process to support the conclusions, another common omission that falls below the standard of practice. As stated above, reconciliation is the final step in the development aspect of the appraisal process, but communicating (reporting) the results is the final step in the appraisal process.

Communicate the Results

The term *communicate the results* refers to reporting the results of the appraisal process. This last step in the appraisal process is sometimes erroneously referred to as the appraisal because the results are generally written in a physical report with a concluded value known as an appraisal. In truth, the appraisal is a process of developing an opinion of value or the opinion of value itself. In other words, the physical report does not in and of itself constitute an appraisal. It is the process and the value conclusion that make the report an appraisal. The validity and credibility of the appraisal are measured by the accuracy of data, the appropriateness of methods and techniques applied, and the soundness of claims made and conclusions reached and supported by the evidence uncovered and presented. This holds true for any assignment type, not just for appraisal assignments.

The Final Step in the Appraisal Process

Throughout this curriculum, we have discussed the importance of keeping the processes within the appraisal process interrelated. Perhaps nowhere is there a greater risk of disconnection within the appraisal process than in the final step of reporting the assignment results. Because developing and reporting are two distinct parts of the same process, there is a potential for a gap between the two steps. While reconciliation is considered to be final step in development, it really is the conduit between development and reporting. Reconciliation is the basis for synthesizing the most relevant points of the analysis to reach opinions and conclusions that will be highlighted within the report. In short, reconciliation contains the relevant information that needs to be effectively communicated within the report.

Effective communication plays a large role in reporting to be sure, but accurately communicating the assignment results is the starting point of proper reporting. Depending on the assignment type, the reporting phase should also reflect what has transpired throughout the appraisal assignment beginning with problem identification and moving through the market analysis steps of subject analysis, market delineation and neighborhood identification, supply and demand analysis, and conclusions. The point is that the communication of results takes place only after the appraisal process has reached conclusions, and that such communication is properly executed based on the client's needs and the complexity of the assignment.

Before we proceed, let's take a moment to break down the appraisal process itself and place this course into perspective. It is critically important that we take the time to address this point to give you an understanding of why the course is required in this curriculum in the first place. Recently, several appraisal underwriters and review appraisers were queried and it was determined that the major problem with real estate appraisal reports is that the appraisers stop speaking like appraisers when it comes to the report function. The language, terms, techniques, and concepts of real estate appraisal are sometimes forgotten or not properly utilized when it comes to the reporting function. This is unforgivable!

To take valuable time and effort at considerable cost to sit through an appraisal curriculum and not implement what you learn is a failure to your status as a professional. For this reason alone, we would like to reiterate the appraisal process and the importance of critical thinking and discuss how the focus of this course fits into your learning experience. As you shall see, the critical thought process is the basis for gaining agreement with your report from the reader.

Keep in mind that although the course isolates certain portions of the appraisal process or individual processes in detail, the intent here is to allow you to become knowledgeable and proficient in the function of these processes, and not to see them as separate functions. Let us remind you about the importance of thinking critically. This will be discussed later in this lesson.

When a process such as highest and best use, critical thought, or scope of work is isolated, you should reflect on how this information fits into the entire appraisal process. You should also reflect on how these processes overlap or interrelate, and finally, you should reflect on how you will report these overlaps.

We know that as a scientific method, the appraisal process begins with identifying a problem and ends with reaching valid conclusions. But what about the ending portion of the process? This final step in the appraisal process is the focus of this course. While we will focus specifically on the reporting of what took place during the development of the appraisal assignment, it is extremely important that your focus be directed toward the effects on the entire assignment, even while focusing on the details of these portions. To see the development and reporting portions as separate and unrelated steps within the appraisal process is to risk loss of validity and therefore credibility, which is a violation of *USPAP*.

Our goal has been to elevate the profession by elevating the professional, but we need your help. As a professional you have obligations and responsibilities—as an appraisal student you have the same. Please think about how you will use this information in practice.

The balance of this course will focus on the final portion of the appraisal process (as outlined in Figure 1.1) with concentration on market analysis, highest and best use, and scope of work, including the critical thought process and concluding with application case studies. As practicing appraisers and real estate appraisal educators, we have tried to bring the field into the classroom, and the classroom into the field. As you know, professionalism is a constant achievement that must be attained if public trust is to be preserved.

Critical Thought Process

As part of the cognitive sciences, much has been written about **critical thinking**. Most of what is written reflects a far more academic approach to the science of the mind with a hefty dose of logic and reasoning. For our purposes, the **critical thought process** in its simplest form is thinking independently. When the standard of practice calls for an appraiser to remain impartial, independent, and objective, it is implied that critical thought should be part of the process. In fact, it is reasonable for the client to expect that the appraisal professional will use critical thinking to process all information throughout the assignment.

Outside influences have little to do with how the critical thinker processes information. Information is gathered, analyzed, and synthesized, and opinions or conclusions are made. Does this sound familiar? It should, because critical thought is the template for the scientific method of analysis.

For humans, critical thinking develops at an early age when a child begins to form strong tendencies or beliefs and to reject irrational notions presented by others. Critical thinkers are active thinkers who try to figure things out for themselves. A critical thinker does not passively accept the beliefs of others, nor do they accept unconfirmed information as fact. Critical thinkers thoughtfully form principles of thought and action and they are not unduly influenced by the language of another.

In valuation, critical thought is far less scientific because the appraisal process itself is a scientific method of analysis. The appraisal process, however, does rely on the appraisal professional or market analyst to exercise critical thought. Critical thought is part of the appraisal process and a key component of the performance standard for appraisal professionals. In short, critical thought has a process that also integrates within the appraisal process that all appraisal professionals are required to follow. Critical thought is therefore required as part of any analysis performed within an appraisal practice.

Although in the cognitive sciences critical thinking begins with identifying the problem, this is already done in the appraisal process at the beginning of the appraisal process itself. For the purposes of valuation, therefore, critical thought begins with some kind of data input that is processed into conclusions based on the application of the specialized knowledge and experience of the analyst.

Data

While data collection is a separate step in the appraisal process and the beginning point of market analysis, data in the critical thought process is the input for making valid conclusions. Data can come from many sources and in varied forms.

Facts

Facts are data to be sure, but in valuation, facts are data that has been verified in the market by the analyst. This step of data verification is a requirement under the *Uniform Standards of Professional Appraisal Practice.* Without verification the information is just data that may or may not be true or accurate; their reliability is suspect if it has not been verified. If such data is not verifiable, the appraiser/analyst must disclose this fact and determine if the use of such data would render results that are not credible. Unverified data is unreliable and may lead to conclusions that are suspect.

Relevant Information

Relevant information is fact (verified data) that has been selected by the analyst as most important or relevant to the question or problem being investigated. Not all data that is uncovered and verified is relevant to the assignment or the identified problem within the assignment and therefore falls beyond the scope of the assignment. Knowing what is relevant information and knowing what to include or exclude in the system is critical to the outcome of the assignment. Such knowledge is only garnered through education, knowledge, and experience.

FIGURE 1.2
The Critical Thought Process

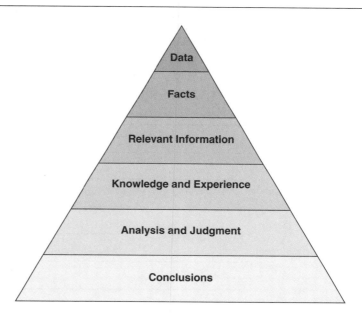

Knowledge and Experience

Knowledge and experience go directly to the Competency provision of the *Uniform Standards of Professional Appraisal Practice.* Competency requires the appraisal professional to know whether he or she is qualified to complete the assignment in a competent manner. Neglecting to perform critical thought is incompetence.

Analysis and Judgment

Proper analysis and judgment come from good data, knowledge, and experience. Analysis is the process of applying critical thought, and judgment is the application of relevant information to the assignment.

Conclusions

Conclusions are supportable decisions or claims that the knowledgeable and experienced analyst determines after collecting and verifying data, selecting relevant information and issues from such data, and applying analysis and judgment to such information. This is all done to answer the key question of problem identification. By now you should recognize this as the scientific method of analysis.

The pyramid in Figure 1.2 depicts how the critical thought process works from placing data into the system to projecting concluded output from the system.

PROFESSIONAL REFLECTION

The appraisal process is comprised of two main parts: developing and reporting.

In the space provided, state *at least* one reason why these two parts should be performed separately. State how these parts are related.

_____

_____

_____

_____

_____

_____

_____

- How does your answer affect assignment accuracy?
- Where is this concern addressed in USPAP?
- Are your answers concerned with critical thought?
- Does your answer include reconciliation?

LESSON 1 REVIEW

1. Critical thought in its simplest form is thinking _____.

2. _____ is the process of giving the most weight to a particular approach over another based on which is most relevant to the problem in order to conclude a final valuation decision.

3. Facts are data that has been _____.

4. Conclusions are _____ decisions or claims.

5. Communicate the results refers to _____ the results of the appraisal process.

6. _____ information is fact that has been selected by the analyst as most important or relevant to the question or problem being investigated.

7. _____ is the process of determining and giving weight to the most relevant information.

8. The appraisal process is a two-part scientific method of _____ and _____.

9. A good management function also includes a(n) _____ mechanism for oversight and for periodically calibrating the manner in which assignments are completed.

10. The information that is required in the problem identification stage is also known as _____.

LESSON 1 REVIEW ANSWERS

1. independently

2. Final reconciliation

3. verified

4. supportable

5. reporting

6. Relevant

7. Reconciliation

8. developing, reporting

9. feedback

10. relevant characteristics

LESSON 2: The Fundamentals of Argumentation

WHAT IS ARGUMENTATION?

What does argumentation mean to you? Very likely your perception of argumentation carries a negative connotation based on what is typically a loud polemic debate. In society today the words *argue* or *argument* suggest an unpleasant quarrelsome experience between two people. Argumentation as a rancorous or bitter exchange is a perversion of the true term and, unfortunately, its meaning has become pejorative in today's society.

It is true that argument seems to be intuitive within human nature; even as children we learn to *argue*. The question is why study this? The answer, very simply, is that a formal understanding of argument will allow us to evaluate and assess arguments. Through a formal study of this natural human activity we will systematically study common sense, and develop a vocabulary that describes this activity so that we can more easily describe and understand what is taking place in the process of arguing. We will therefore be able to make judgments of arguments so that we might improve our performance as creators and analysts of arguments. As makers and analyzers of arguments we can create and maintain productive arguments and understand how claims are made and supported. Note the term *productive arguments* in the previous sentence. What do we mean by productive argument?

We would like you to set aside all of your current stereotypes concerning argument in favor of considering the term in its classic sense. This should suggest that argument has a higher meaning and, indeed, in the classic definition, *argument* is reason giving. Of course the term *reason* also carries with it more than one definition in today's society. For our purposes, reason is a justification for a *claim*. A **claim** is a statement of fact that the advocate asks the audience to accept. You will note that the word *fact* is included in this definition. If the claim is not a fact, then it can easily be dismissed as not relevant or not provable. Of course, it is not a coincidence that fact is what the critical thought process requires to reach conclusions.

If the claim is accepted by all parties, then there is no argument, no point of debate. However, if the claim is not accepted and therefore requires justification, then an argument is created. For this reason it can also be said that arguing is the practice of justifying claims. We will further discuss claims later in this lesson.

Argument, like appraisal, can be a process or a product, and to the knowledgeable, argumentation involves the production and exchange of messages in interaction with other people. The *message* is the product of argumentation. Messages can be produced in almost any form such as verbal, nonverbal, formal text, or otherwise. But a message must be able to be placed into language so as to allow us to examine the message as part of claims and justifications. A message can be explicit or implicit. By this we mean that a message might be expressly stated or implied by something else.

The justification or support for a claim must be connected or *rational;* otherwise, the argument is seen as irrational. For this reason, we say that *rationality* is the ability to engage in reason giving. In fact, what makes us rational is our ability to engage in reason giving based on our ability to connect the claims that we make and the justification for such claims. If there is no connection between the claims that are made and the justification for the claim, then credibility is lost and our argument is dismissed by the audience. Therefore, **argumentation** is the study of *effective* reasoning. You will note that we have emphasized the word *effective*. This should imply to you that there is an audience in mind. Indeed, argumentation is an appeal to a specific audience. The words *specific audience* should suggest that there is a need on the part of the advocate (claim maker) to appeal to a specific reader or audience. In order for such an appeal to be effective, the advocate must seek to impact or influence the audience.

The success of an argument will be measured in the *assent* of the audience. The **assent** is the audience's acceptance or adherence to the claim based upon the reasons given to justify the claim. Therefore, the assent is the audience's acceptance of the reasoning and connection between the justifications and the claim. It is not an automatic acceptance of such claims or the connection between claims and justifications. The audience will apply its knowledge, experience, analysis, and judgment to determine if the conclusions are reasonable. Sound familiar? This should imply that the audience is of a critical mind and that the assent of the audience will not automatically be given to the advocate, until valid reasoning is used to support the claim.

This leads us to another term related to argument called *rhetoric*. Like argument, the term *rhetoric* is pejorative in the way modern society defines it. Today, rhetoric has negative connotations associated with empty, bombastic, and ornamental language. But, of course, the classic definition of rhetoric is quite different. **Rhetoric** is the study of how messages influence people. Rhetoric focuses on the interaction between speaker and audience with particular attention paid to development and communication of knowledge between speakers and listeners. Let us repeat that! The focus of rhetoric is on the development and communication of knowledge between the speaker and the audience. We hope that this sounds familiar, as *development* and *communication* (reporting) are the two-part portions of the appraisal process. How knowledge is developed and communicated is the basic focus of all readers of an appraisal report. So where do argument and rhetoric fit?

Argumentation is in fact a subset of rhetoric. Exploring how people are influenced by reason-giving is what argumentation really attempts to accomplish. But because rhetoric studies the influences of messages it includes more than reason alone. Rhetoric also includes the mechanics of style, presentation, language, emotional appeals, verbal and nonverbal influences of the message, and so on. So when it is said to "think rhetorically," the inference is to think about the intended audience. **Rhetorical thinking,** then, is thinking about the audience, the predispositions of the audience, and the process of reasoning made in the argument that would have an influence on the audience.

The History of Argument and Rhetoric

Argumentation as a study is over 2,500 years old and dates back to 500 BC to ancient Greek philosophers. While the intelligentsia, or philosophical class, within ancient Greece practiced various forms of debate, it was not until there was a political reason for the general society to concern itself with such activity that argumentation and rhetoric became mainstream.

Around 389 BC, a tyrant by the name of Thrasybulus of Syracuse was overthrown, and the properties that where confiscated during his tyrannical rule were offered to be returned to the original owners under the new democratic regime. The only thing that needed to be done was that the original owner needed to "claim" the property and argue for its return. The problem was that most people had no idea how to present a claim that would unequivocally convince the audience. From this societal need came a group of intellectuals called *Sophists*. Sophists were a class of people who understood the rules of argumentation. Sophists began teaching the rules of presentation and argument as a means of helping the rightful owners stake claim to the properties. Of course, sophistry as it is known today also has negative connotations of empty and fancy speech, which is of little value. However, in ancient Greek society the Sophists were a very respectable and well-educated class. In fact, an early Sophist named Protagoras (circa 445 BC) is often regarded as "the father of debate."

The biggest critic of the Sophists was Plato (428–347 BC), who dismissed the Sophists as being only concerned with presentation style and winning and unconcerned with the truth of an argument. To Plato, the Sophists were too dependent upon rhetoric, which was all about convincing an audience with techniques of appearances. He believed that the Sophists would make the lesser argument seem stronger, and that winning the debate was a more desirable outcome than reaching the essence of what would be regarded as the truths behind the case. Plato, a man of philosophy, further contended that these excesses were inherent in the subject of rhetoric. Philosophy was more concerned with the thought or reasoning toward the truth behind a case, while rhetoric was more concerned about the use of appearances to convince an audience.

It is important to note that because of their excessive and primary concern for appearances, the Sophists lost credibility with Plato first and then with Greek society as a whole. While Plato's indictment of the entire profession was likely unfair to some within the profession of sophistry, the excessive concern with appearances is how public trust is lost. At first it is a few negligent practitioners that reflect upon the entire profession, then the entire profession turns towards negligence either by action or by reputation, and public trust is lost. When public trust is lost, so too is the need for the profession.

In our book *Basic Appraisal Principles,* the curriculum opens with a discussion entitled "What Is a Profession?" It is reprinted here with some basic points about professionalism.

What Is a Profession?

There are three essential criteria that help to establish a profession when compared with a trade or other such skills of labor:

1. There must be a code of ethics and a clearly defined standard by which the professional must practice. This is known as the *standard of practice* in a given field of professional endeavor.

2. There must be a quantified level of *qualification* through education and experience. This is normally achieved through licensing and/or certification.

3. There must be a continued dedication toward acquisition and maintenance of the *public trust* (credibility maintained through competency).

The first two points are rather obvious, but the last and, undoubtedly, the most important point concerning public trust might not be so clear. Since the public trust is maintained within the heart of every individual in a given profession, such trust might be abused should the actions of the individual professional fail to perform to a standard requisite of the profession. Having a code of ethics and a clearly identified standard under which the professional must practice is known as the standard of practice. But this is only half of the equation. The practice standard must be maintained individually (by each appraiser) and collectively (by the profession as a whole).

Further, should those within a profession that are responsible for the continued monitoring and enforcement of the standards fail to do so, abuses are sure to occur. When such abuses become commonplace, either by poor individual performance, or by the lack of oversight and enforcement, then public trust is seriously depleted, or even nonexistent, and the entire profession suffers.

Little by little the Sophists chipped away at the foundation of the profession by not maintaining a standard of practice and by not having a system of oversight in place to uphold the standards. Because the standard of practice in sophistry fell below society's needs and expectations, and since appearances became more important to the Sophists than reality or what we call "gaining the truth of an argument," credibility for the profession and therefore the profession itself was lost.

Nowhere in the appraisal profession is there greater ability for appearances to be crafted that are not based in reality than in report writing. But a well-trained reviewer or appraisal professional will know what to look for within another appraiser's work. With proper analysis techniques, any report can be scrutinized for accuracy and soundness of conclusions. This is our point in studying argumentation, the appraisal process, and the details of reporting. To help each individual achieve excellence with every report drafted according to an acceptable standard of practice.

The Sophists failed to maintain and monitor such standards, and their entire profession suffered because of it! Plato carried a great deal of weight and respect during his tenure, and his denouncement of the Sophists certainly meant negative consequences for the profession. Because the Sophists depended so heavily on rhetoric, and since the philosophical-minded Plato also denounced rhetoric, this too should have meant the demise of rhetoric as a field of study. But it was Aristotle (384–322 BC) who revived rhetoric, believing that the practice of studying audience persuasion was worth pursuing. Aristotle recognized that it was the performance of the Sophists (pardon the pun) that lead to their demise, but that rhetoric was valid.

In 350 BC, Aristotle wrote a book titled *The Rhetoric* claiming the benefits of rhetorical thought and the concepts behind the study of rhetoric. Aristotle perfected the concept of rhetoric and defined the term as "the skill of discovering the available means of persuasion in a given case." The term "means" is quite obviously extended beyond the term "reason" within the basic definition of argument. Remember, argumentation is the study of effective reasoning, while rhetoric is the study of persuading an audience. So to Aristotle, the means of convincing were as important as the reasons for convincing an audience.

Because of Aristotle's discourse on rhetoric, the subject became one of the seven classical liberal arts. The traditional seven liberal arts were as follows:

1. Grammar

2. Logic/dialectic

3. Rhetoric

4. Arithmetic

5. Geometry

6. Music

7. Astronomy

Further, rhetoric was seen well through the period of the Roman Empire as a skill required by the *good citizen orator* of Rome. It was commonly accepted that every citizen should learn to speak well and influence others through the formal skill of rhetoric and rhetorical thought. Rhetoric in the Roman era was used for pedagogical or formal teaching purposes.

Commerce was the order of the day during the Roman Empire and rhetoric was accepted as part of a liberal arts education with the fundamental canons based in teaching. These *five canons* are important as the basis of knowledge sharing even today:

1. **Invention**—The process of discovery. To find the available resources to be used and to select the proper information. You might have recognized this as the development portion of the appraisal process, the beginning portion of the scientific method, and the first few steps of the critical thought process whereby relevant information is identified and used.

2. **Arrangement**—The pattern of organization and the parts of a speech. Indeed, the Romans were the earliest to work on the patterns of organization. What should be done in each part and how the parts should work as a whole for persuasive purposes. You will recognize this as developing a thought by creating a sentence, placing the sentence within a paragraph, and so forth. This is indeed the reporting portion of the appraisal process or scientific method.

3. **Style**—The use of language. Using different language to convince different audiences. To select words and phrases that would resonate with the audience. The tone used in language and to what level.

4. **Memory**—The process of keeping in mind what one would say. This is *not* concerned with memorization, but is concerned with keeping in mind the elements of an appeal. To be capable of recalling one's own points in order of importance or keeping an inventory of your opponent's points so as to be able to rebut those points when your turn to speak was at hand.

5. **Delivery**—The physical presentation. The use of voice, body, gestures, and so on.

Rhetoric remained a highly desired formal skill through the medieval period where religion was the order of the day, and within the Church rhetoric became the basis for preaching and teaching. You might have already noted that if you take the first two canons *invention* and *arrangement* and placed them together, you have something akin to argumentation. As the medieval period progressed, argumentation became a process of identifying what would be used for appeals and determining how to place this information together in an orderly structure. This is significant because here is where the evolution of rhetoric and argument will ultimately force a splitting of the two and lead to modern society's misunderstanding of both.

It was during the early Renaissance when an otherwise obscure philosopher named Peter Ramus (1515–1572) bifurcated the canons associated with invention and arrangement and placed them in the field of philosophy and defined rhetoric as style, memory, and delivery. This rendered rhetoric less of an intellectual function and more of a physical function dealing with gestures, speech, and other such stylistic devices. Ramus's division implied that the process of discovering what was true was different from the presentation of what was true. Ramus took apart what Aristotle had placed together. You might have already discerned that this was precisely Plato's point about rhetoric used in sophistry—that technique was more important than substance and that the public was easily fooled by a case presented well even though it lacked substance.

Pause for Reflection

This leads us to the question, Can an appraisal report be written in such a way that it "looks good" but lacks substance? Can this type of activity lead to our professional downfall if the general public loses trust in our work?

The answer is that, unfortunately, this sort of thing takes place everyday, whether intentional or not, and it damages us all as appraisal professionals. This is why verification of data is so important to the critical thought process as well. Support for an argument has to be made with verified evidence.

René Descartes (1596–1650) would ponder the question of human knowledge and develop the philosophical statement, "I think therefore I am." This famous statement was Descartes's response to the question, What can you know?

Descartes believed that we should all systematically doubt everything. Further, Descartes challenged philosophers to accept as true only what could be shown to be self-evident. This Cartesian revolution of philosophy, as it has been called, was marked by the quest to only reason from self-evident premises or from certainty.

When philosophy takes on a requirement of certainty then invention and arrangement are worthless. The result has been that these important canons were lost on philosophical thought until the 19th century. Reasoning therefore becomes identified with the study of *formal logic* alone. Before we move forward, we must provide two other terms that are related fields of study: *logic* and *dialectic.*

Logic is concerned with all forms and structures of **reasoning.** Unfortunately, logic is sometimes mistakenly thought of as being only related to formal reasoning, which means symbolic (as in the use of symbols) or mathematical reasoning. As such, logic is erroneously thought of as having only a certainty of outcome using *symbolic formulas* such as those that are conducted according to mathematical or statistical modeling.

The truth is that logic is concerned with all forms of reasoning whether formal or not. Because of this notion, philosophy and argumentation have seen a rise in *informal logic,* which is grounded in ordinary language and describes a reasoning pattern that lacks the certainty of mathematics. This new field of study, called *informal logic,* is closely related to what we would call the traditional or classic definition of argumentation where reasoning does not have certainty.

In argumentation, which is defined as reason giving, we are searching for the truth to the argument, or at least the likelihood of truth. *Formal logic* or *formal reasoning* has become so structured and dependent upon certainty that it is limited in its applicability and not well suited for our purposes of engaging in the type of reasoning required in argumentation. In contrast, informal logic offers the proper structures of reasoning required as a model for the argumentation we require in our profession so that we might reach supportable conclusions. As appraisal professionals, we must test the knowledge provided as support for our conclusions, and *dialectic reasoning* is related to this process.

The term **dialectic** is the process of using questions and answers to discover or test knowledge. The *Socratic Method* is a method developed by Plato and perfected by Socrates whereby the two advocates seek the answer to a question by asking a series of questions surrounding the central issue. Notice that the two advocates are working in conjunction with one another to seek the answer as a truth to the question. This is considerably different than the pejorative notion of argumentation in today's society. The advocates seek to reach the truth as a common goal by the exchange of thoughts, claims, and questions.

At this point, you might be asking yourself, What does a two-way debate between opposing advocates asking questions of one another as a challenge of claims have to do with appraisal report writing? This is a fair question. The answer, quite frankly, is that the drafter of an appraisal report is required to provide information that is relevant to the assignment, with opinions and conclusions that are supported. Asking pertinent questions of oneself during the development stage of an assignment and challenging one's own observations, opinions, and conclusions so that they stand up to scrutiny is essential to providing evidence in support of such claims made in the reporting stage of an assignment. This is the basis of critical thought in the appraisal process.

So how do these terms all interrelate? It can be said that argumentation is the field of study where rhetoric, logic, and dialectic all meet. Argumentation is reason-giving, rhetoric is the study of persuading an audience, logic is the structure behind the reasoning, and dialectic is the process of testing the knowledge with questions.

We are happy to note that during the 20th and 21st centuries there has been a developing concern for what the approach to formal reasoning has left out. This growing concern has created a revolution in movement from certainty in argument to probability. The concern is that to argue only from certainty does not allow for the delving into the complexities of modern life and, as we have said, formal reasoning is not a suitable model for reaching the likely truths in such issues.

Pause for Reflection

At this point, we must ask the question, Is the valuation of real estate or real property an activity that deals in certainty or probability; and which form of logic is more appropriate for reason giving in valuation?

The answer is that markets are not absolute certainties; therefore, informal reasoning is more conducive to developing and reporting the results of an appraisal assignment, particularly when dialectic questioning is used to challenge the information.

While it may seem that other than providing a few specific philosophical terms we have thus far professed nothing new concerning argumentation, it should be clear that we are moving toward some sort of specialized knowledge base. When considering together the appraisal process, the critical thought process, rhetoric, and argument, the basis for communicating and the requirements for reporting are suggested. The appraisal process develops and reports on the development of opinions and conclusion based on the data, facts, and relevant information uncovered in market analysis, highest and best use analysis, and the approaches to value after applying the critical thought process. The concept of rhetoric, which is to convince an audience about the claims made in the opinions and conclusions section of the assignment, is really the goal of the argument made in favor of those conclusions.

As a review, we have suggested that you cast aside the pejorative notion of argument as a bitter exchange between people and instead focus on the classic view of argument as a practice of giving reasons to justify claims while seeking the adherence of an audience. When viewed from this perspective, argumentation is indeed part of the human condition. From this view, argumentation is something in which we participate all of the time. We engage in argumentation almost anytime that we possess a point of view or seek to influence another person or group of people on some level. Yet, argumentation as a formal study and part of an education curriculum on any level from grammar school to graduate studies is a rarity in our society. But it seems that civility is as well.

Perhaps if a formal study of argumentation was required within the curriculum of our educational system there would be more thought-provoking leaders in our society and true statesmen in government. There would undoubtedly be better written and more thought-provoking material than now exists in what passes for intellectual forums throughout our educational system.

Because the general consensus in our society supports the notion that argumentation is something that is a natural part of human activity, and therefore does not need to be formally taught, we seem to have lost the ability in general to engage in a civilized debate. However the difference between productive arguments, which are those that present claims and provide reasons to support such claims, and arguments that are quarrelsome or unproductive and invoke the negative stereotypes is what we call argumentation.

So where do we see evidence of argumentation in modern life? In what forum is there conflict or an adversarial environment in which the truth or at least the probability of discovering the truth can be engaged? In this country, that evidence can be found in the court system. The two advocates—plaintiff and defendant—state their case, ask questions of witnesses, challenge the evidence, and make their appeal to the trier-of-fact. The absolute truth may not be unequivocally known, but the probability of the truth "beyond a reasonable doubt" is where the decision is likely to rest. Because there can be errors made throughout the case and bad decisions rendered, our courts have an appeals process to help insulate against poor judgment or decisions made based on erroneous evidence or faulty procedures.

It is worth noting that the legal term *trier-of-fact*, which refers to the judge, jury, arbitrator, or mediator in a case, has the word *fact* in the title. You will recall that the critical thought process requires data to be verified to fact and facts that are relevant are deemed relevant information under the critical thought process. This relevant information is what should be submitted as evidence of an argument in a case.

Just like irrational arguments, a case presented without relevant facts should be dismissed. Remember that if the claims made are not connected in a rational way or make no sense to the case, then the argument is dismissed as irrational. The same holds true for relevant information. The advocate might present facts, but those facts must be relevant to the case and connected in a way that allows the audience to give its assent. If the facts are not relevant, then the point made and perhaps the entire argument are dismissed as irrelevant.

By now you should be grasping the specialized knowledge base to which we alluded earlier. You should be internalizing that rhetoric, which is the process of convincing an audience of the truths uncovered in a case, is what report writing is all about. Rhetoric recognizes that there is room for uncertainty in an argument, which benefits your claim when interpreting the nuances of a market. Markets are not certain and, as such, any claims made about the market can be and should be challenged. But to make claims that have been vetted with the question and answering process of dialectics is what every report writing appraisal professional is required to do during the development portion of the appraisal process. These facts, questions, and answers should be challenged *before* reconciliation is performed and the report is drafted.

Dialectics recognizes that there are cases where there are no absolute answers. This fits well with market analysis because markets are curious and complex. Because of their complexity, markets are difficult to predict with certainty. Yet, within an uncertain world, dialectics recognizes and allows for the consideration, investigation, and conclusions based on the probability of certainty.

Dialectics helps to discern the truth or essence of something in situations where there is no absolute answer and where claims about things are uncertain, which means that they could be otherwise but are supposed for the purpose of argument, and with the intention of testing the validity of a claim as a means of sorting through to the likely truth of the matter. Through careful questioning, analysis, and synthesis, a claim can be accepted even if it is not certain; "if" the reason for making the claim is rational, factual, and relevant then the claim should be accepted at least as possible if not probable. And what is the basis of market value? "The *probable* price . . ."

So how do we decide whether to think this or that, or whether this is possible, probable, or unlikely? How do we decide that a claim is reasonable, rational, and relevant? We do so by critical examination through questions and answers. We engage in dialectics using the critical thought process whereby we question the facts, opinions, and conclusions using our knowledge and experience and analysis and judgment as background for our acceptance or rejection of the claims made. If we are the drafter of such claims then we must appeal to an audience as if the same process is to be performed. In short, we suggest that you complete every assignment "as if it is going to court," because it just might! Your work will be scrutinized by your peers and this process of critical thought should be seriously considered before you draft your report.

Argumentation and the Scientific Method

Argumentation is a process that is analogous to the scientific method, as their purposes are similar. Both seek to find truths that were otherwise unknown and to investigate what we should believe to be true about matters that are inherently uncertain.

Science is the rigorous testing of something that is empirical (that which can be measured with certainty), which means that in scientific studies something is being tested that is expected to be measured with certainty. This is why a hypothesis is used within the scientific method in scientific research. The hypothesis is drafted based on what is already known and attempts go beyond that which is known to discover new truths through scientific testing. The hypothesis becomes the focus of the experiment, or research study, to prove, disprove, or measure something related to the issue within the hypothesis.

Argumentation is a testing of the nonempirical (that which is not certain). In argumentation, things are not subject to certainty as in formal logic. Argumentation is an attempt to reach a relative certainty in an area of study where certainty is not possible. Like scientific study, argumentation begins with what is known and attempts to go beyond the known to discover the likely truths about what is uncertain.

Pause for Reflection

If appraisers use the scientific method known as the appraisal process but do not develop a hypothesis as in scientific research, what then takes the place of a hypothesis in the appraisal process? Give an example of your answer.

Answer: The purpose of the assignment with the defined problem stated in the problem identification step of the appraisal process.

Example: "To determine the market value of the subject for mortgage consideration." You will note that this is the basis of the scope of work decision in an assignment.

The focus is on the probable based on the uncovering of such likely truths. This is why we do not use a hypothesis in the appraisal process, and why you should not allow any preconceived notions to leach into your thought process during the execution of an assignment. The market must speak for itself! An appraiser must remain independent, impartial, and objective and allow the market data to speak for itself. Critically analyzing the relevant information and accurately interpreting this information to reach valid conclusions is what the appraisal professional should be doing in an assignment.

The arguers (advocates) are performing a role similar to a scientific researcher in a laboratory. As appraisers performing the appraisal process through research and developing arguments to support our conclusions, we are executing a similar function to that of the scientific researcher seeking the truths to a hypothesis. In our case we do not have a hypothesis, but a purpose of the assignment to answer the identified and defined problem. This defined problem is really the basis of scope of work.

Argumentation, a Microview

So what are the mechanics of argumentation? As we stated, argumentation is *not* a confrontational exercise. While there is an element of adversarial interaction between opposing advocates, the relationship as a whole should be thought of as a challenging of the information presented; a cooperative dialogue attempting to reach the truth of the matter. The view about argumentation should be more toward settling a controversy rather than committing to a cause or being an adversary pitted against the opposing advocate. This leads us to yet another term: *controversy*. And yes, like most of the terms already presented, controversy has a slightly different meaning in the field of argumentation than its colloquial definition would imply.

In argumentation, **controversy** is the context in which the argument takes place. As explained earlier, reasons are justifications for claims. If the claim is accepted by all parties, then there is no argument, no point of debate. However, if the claim is not accepted and requires justification, then an argument is created within this controversy. Aristotle wrote, "On matters which are certain no one deliberates." We deliberate (argue) when there is *not* an easier way to resolve the dispute or disagreement.

Once there is a controversy from which to argue, people will engage in argumentation (reason giving) to support their view. An emergence of controversy is not in and of itself a bad thing. Controversy exposes things to other possibilities and different viewpoints. The following conditions must exist before people will deliberate and for there to be a productive argument:

- There must be a disagreement between the two parties.

- There must be a controversy in the mind of the two parties, and the issue must matter to the two parties.

- Both parties must desire to resolve the dispute.

- Both parties must seek the assent of the other or a third party that will decide the case. (This openly shows respect for the other party's judgment.)

- Both parties must be willing to freely give their assent if the other party presents a compelling case.

  - By freely giving or receiving the assent of the other, both parties recognize that this builds confidence in the argument particularly in matters that are uncertain.

  - This also reflects a desire to get to the truth of the matter even if one's own case is proved to be incorrect.

- There are no easier means of resolving the dispute. If there is no way to resolve the dispute, then the two parties will deliberate, but only after first testing the following methods of resolution:

  - *Empirical method*—As an example, if we were to dispute how many people are signed up for this course we would simple count the number of people. This would quite easily resolve the dispute.

  - *Universally recognized authority*—If there is a source that is recognized by both parties as an authority on the matter they would simply consult this authority to settle the dispute.

  - *Deductive method*—If both parties could reach conclusions from something that they already know, then they could deduce an answer and find an agreement.

Argumentation is in fact a cooperative event in which the two parties are working toward a resolution of the disagreement. If the advocate states a belief and makes a claim that supports the belief, and if the claim or the argument is shown to be wrong, then both parties should agree and that should be the end of it; in a perfect world that is the case.

The question then becomes, if both parties are in agreement about the event, where does argumentation go wrong? The answer is that, aside from the obvious issue that most people lack an understanding of what argument is or should be and therefore do not how to correctly engage in an argument, argumentation calls for each advocate to take a risk.

- The advocate risks being wrong.

  - This strikes the ego and sometimes hurts.

  - Being wrong is unsettling and raises doubt in one's abilities.

  - Being wrong might diminish community or professional status.

- The advocate risks his or her belief system.

  - One might have to change one's beliefs, and we know how well human nature accepts change!

So why then does one take on such risks by making an argument? Because it is important to the advocate, and resolving the dispute might lead to a deeper and more accurate understanding of the issues, particularly if certainty is not possible. Further, we seek the assent of the other advocate as a means of solidifying or validating our claims and argument. In effect, gaining adherence or assent from a critical listener such as the opposing advocate is a close substitute for gaining certainty when absolute certainty is not possible. This builds confidence in our own arguments and supports the probability of being correct.

■ In Practice

A review appraiser or underwriter sends a query to your office concerning something within the appraisal report that you drafted. Your immediate reaction as an appraisal professional should be

a. outrage that the idiot does not immediately understand your point.

b. to take the time to listen to the essence of the misunderstanding.

c. to recognize the queries as part of the process and give further clarification.

d. Both b and c

While it is obvious that the best way to handle such a query is to first understand the nature of the question and then work in a cooperative effort to clarify the problem, some appraisers see such queries as a challenge to their judgment. Like we said, human nature is a funny thing, especially when ego is involved.

Recognize that the query was launched because you may not have provided a sound argument in your reporting or that you have either poorly described the issue or not properly addressed a concern. It could be that you have provided a report that is potentially misleading, which is a potential violation of standard rules.

You have an obligation to remain professional throughout the appraisal process, even after the report is delivered.

The role of critical listener is yet another way in which argumentation is seen as a cooperative event. By listening to the claims and answers to the questions, a critical listener has the obligation to either accept or reject the claim or the evidence presented. In argumentation there is mutual contribution whereby the truth of the matter is tested and the argument is strengthened, or perhaps a new argument is developed. Either way, we are getting closer to the truth through this process.

This means that there must be a common language amongst advocates so as to ensure that they are not "speaking past each other," which means that they are not arguing about the same point. So while there are many more terms to be had within argumentation, we are only going to concern this course with those that are related to our purposes as appraisal professionals.

We have already discussed how claims are made, but let's be clear as to why claims are made. Recall that a claim is a statement of fact that the advocate asks the audience to accept.

The advocate must use claims to gain the assent or adherence of the audience to persuade the audience to agree with the advocate's opinions and conclusions. Such adherence must be acquired by using facts and logical reasoning.

Any controversy can be seen as posing a major question, and a claim is an attempt to convince the audience to accept the advocate's answer to that question. We already used the term resolution as a means of identifying what the advocates are attempting to find as the truth to the case, or to find a point of agreement. In fact, the **resolution** is the *ultimate* claim that an advocate attempts to prove or disprove; it is the very substance of the argument. A resolution should be able to be given in the form of a declarative statement that captures the essence of what the controversy is about. The resolution answers the question in a controversy. It might not put the matter to rest, but it will be the ground on which the advocates will decide whether to accept the statement embodied within the resolution.

Keeping in mind that in a case where the audience is using critical analysis and the claim made is rejected, the audience might actually take on the role of an opposing advocate. In this instance, the audience will place its arguments against the claim on the resolution where the disagreement lies. Remember the ultimate goal of argument is to convince the audience, even if the audience is an opposing advocate. Through presenting claims and giving evidence to support the claims, both parties engage in productive dialogue as an attempt to convince the other side of the merits of their argument, and thus find ground on which to agree. This is what is meant by gaining assent and getting to the truth of the matter.

Pause for Reflection

As an example:

The controversy is to ask:

"What is the market value of the subject property?"

The resolution is:

"The property is worth $250,000."

How we came to this conclusion is not yet clear. But we certainly understand the focus of the case on which we must decide to agree or not.

The controversy and the resolution are directly stated and all parties can easily understand the significant points to be addressed.

Before a productive argument can be executed, both parties must agree on the topic about which they are disagreeing. Otherwise, the advocates will likely argue past each other, not engaging each other or arguing different points. Remember, an argument is reason giving and the controversy is the context in which the argument takes place, which means that there must be a mutual question from which the argument is executed.

As we can see, something has to take place to get from the essence of the controversy to the resolution. Aside from requiring the assent of the audience, some sort of dialogue must take place to support the resolution.

The question becomes, What do we need to establish the resolution? The answer is found in the term *issue*. And of course issue is a very broad term in today's society, and typically means any sort of disagreement as in "these two have issues with each other." But, of course, in argumentation the definition of issue is quite different.

In argumentation, an **issue** is the question or the argument (reasons) that is inherent in the controversy and required to reach the resolution. The issue is vital to establishing the grounds on which the argument will take place so that the claims can be made and so that the resolution can be reached.

Pause for Reflection

Using the example in the previous Pause for Reflection, what are the issues involved with the resolution of the controversy of what is the market value of the subject property?

Answer: The market data and analysis, highest and best use, and the three approaches to value.

So you see that the issues are implicit within the controversy and that resolution follows naturally from the controversy.

If there are a series of issues needed to get to the resolution, then each is separate and challengeable. Sometimes more proof is needed to support a resolution because of the complexity or uncertainty of the case.

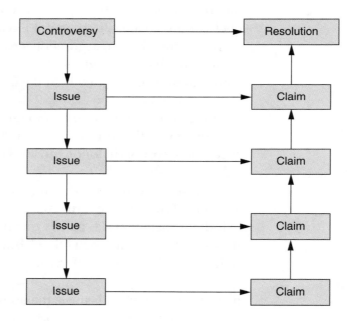

■ In Practice

Suppose we completed three approaches to value for the above-mentioned property noted in the Pause for Reflection. Given the following, draw an illustration identifying the controversy, the resolutions, the issues, and the claims:

The sales comparison approach concluded a value of $250,000.

The cost approach concluded a value of $249,000.

The income approach concluded a value of $248,000.

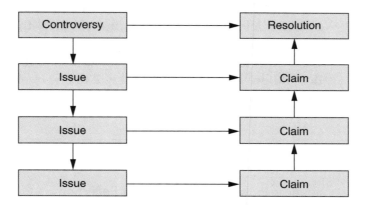

Solution:

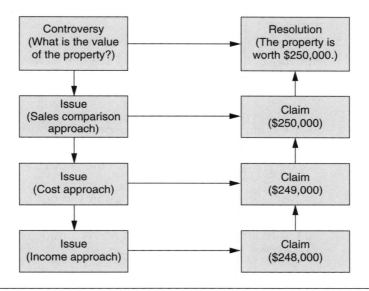

This leads us to another term known as *case,* which we have already used with some regularity. In argumentation, a *case* is the overall structure of an argument using *evidence* that is developed to support or to oppose the resolution. Think first about the critical thought process and the appraisal process and the definition of case is quite clear. Think how a critical thinker would look at the previous illustration and determine if adherence to the resolution that the property is worth $250,000 would be given.

As stated, a case is the structure of the argument using *evidence* that is developed to support or oppose the resolution. You will note the significance of the word *developed.* This is the beginning portion of the appraisal process, which is where evidence is collected. The question now becomes, what is to be considered as *evidence* in a case? In argumentation, **evidence** is a statement that is offered as support for a claim.

In the critical thought process, relevant information is data that has been verified to fact and deemed to be relevant to the assignment in some way. In short, relevant information in the critical thought process is really evidence to support the claims that are made. Just like relevant information in the critical thought process, evidence has to first be relevant to the resolution, otherwise audience assent will not be freely given to the advocate. An irrelevant fact is still not considered to be evidence in a case.

■ In Practice

Suppose in the previous Pause for Reflection we found that the house had a blue door. This is fact, but is it relevant to the resolution that the property is worth $250,000?

Solution:

Probably not. The audience would see this fact as not rising to the level of evidence that would support the resolution that has concluded a value indication of $250,000.

Since it is not likely that the blue door on the house is what determines the value, this fact is irrelevant and, therefore, not considered to be evidence. The blue door is fact, but it is not evidence to support the value conclusion.

Likewise, providing a value conclusion without using recognized methods and techniques or simply providing a value conclusion without support is akin to "pulling the information out of thin air," and is considered a violation of the standard of practice.

Pause for Reflection

This leads us to a point of professional courtesy that we would like to emphasize early on in your career.

At one point or another as you develop specialized knowledge and understanding for the appraisal profession, you will no doubt be asked to perform a review on another appraiser's work. Standard 3 of the *Uniform Standards of Professional*

(continued)

Appraisal Practice covers both the developing and reporting of an appraisal review assignment and the standard is quite clear about your task as a review appraiser. While the standard of practice is clearly defined within Standard 3, we would like to emphasize your professional responsibility to this standard, but with a suggestion for professional courtesy. Simply because you have been engaged to review a report drafted by another professional appraiser does not in and of itself imply that there are any problems within the report. Often, mortgage lenders have a quality control requirement whereby a certain number of reports are randomly selected for review.

May we suggest that your attitude as a professional dedicated to the field of valuation review be conducted under the following premise:

The work you are about to review is the result of another professional's endeavors. Further, this appraiser is a licensed or certified professional belonging to the same field in which you are currently engaged and, as such, this person deserves the presumption of professional courtesy by which all professionals should be judged.

You should enter this assignment with the expectation of professional conduct and presumption of proper performance conducted by our colleague. In other words, you should grant this appraiser the benefit of the doubt until this appraiser has proved himself or herself unworthy of such benefit. At that point you should work to remove this person from our midst because poor performance is an abuse of public trust and a reflection on us all!

On the other hand, proper performance should be openly praised!

In valuation, a resolution of value involves critical judgment. If there is an absence of controversy in that the audience freely gives its assent to the advocate's case then *presumption* prevails. A **presumption** is that which the audience will presume (or assume) about the case unless or until it is shown to be otherwise. If the audience finds no reason to challenge the case, then the presumption is made by the audience that the advocate is correct. This does not mean that the advocate *is* correct; it simply means that the audience has not challenged the case and thus there is no controversy. If the audience successfully challenges the advocate, in that the case or something within the case is shown to be wrong, then the presumption changes to the new found truth. This is how presumption might shift.

An appraisal decision must reach an absolute resolution, which means that the conclusion must be supported with some claim that is further supported by evidence. In other words, the proof requirement for such claims is higher and requires evidence to support the claim. The responsibility to support the resolution or claims made in the resolution falls on the advocate. This is known as *burden of proof*. The **burden of proof** is the ultimate responsibility to support one's resolution or claims in a given case. So how does one prove their case? With evidence.

If the claim is immediately accepted then there is no argument. But if the claim is not immediately accepted then evidence to support the argument is required. The mental movement from evidence to claim so that one accepts the evidence is called **inference**. The inference can be thought of as the rationale of the evidence; the connection between the evidence and the claim.

■ In Practice

Suppose an advocate states that we are heading into a recession and cites that "the stock market is weakening" as the evidence given to support the claim. Illustrate this relationship. Identify the inference with a statement!

The stock market is weakening. We are heading into a recession.

Inference: A weakening of the stock market is an indication of recessionary times ahead.

If the evidence is challenged, then further evidence is required to support the evidence that supports the claim. Let us illustrate:

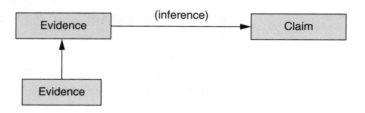

■ In Practice

Suppose that the evidence is challenged because the audience does not believe that the stock market is weakening. Suppose that the Dow Jones, the Mercantile Exchange, and the Nasdaq all fell. Illustrate this relationship. Identify the inference with a statement.

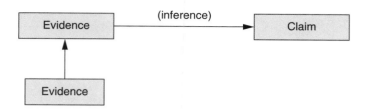

Solution:

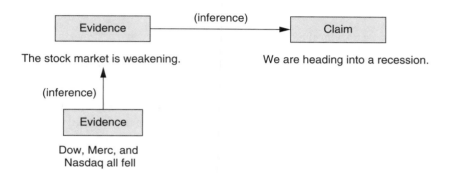

New inference: The Dow, Merc, and Nasdaq are indicators of the stock market.

Suppose that the inference is challenged and not the evidence. Then a warrant is required to support the inference. A **warrant** is the support for making an inference.

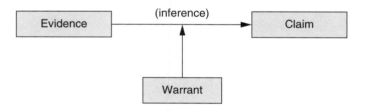

■ **In Practice**

Suppose that the inference is challenged because the audience does not believe that a weakening stock market is an indication of recessionary times ahead.

Suppose that throughout history it could be shown that all recessions were preceded by a weakened stock market. Support the inference with the warrant and illustrate this relationship. Identify the warrant with a statement.

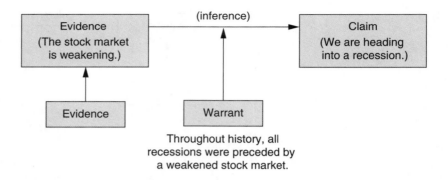

Claims are used as support of the **resolution** that answers the controversy. Of course, the controversy is the central question or what we would refer to as the purpose of the assignment based on the identified problem of the assignment. So, it is fair to say that a properly drafted report is really a case for your argument supporting your opinion and conclusions. We would like to reiterate our suggestion that you write each report as if it is going to court, because it just might. This leads us to one final question: "How strong is your case?"

LESSON 2 REVIEW QUESTIONS

1. _____ are justifications for claims.

2. _____ is reason giving.

3. Rationality is the _____ to engage in reason giving.

4. The assent is the audience's acceptance of or adherence to the claim based upon the reasons given to justify the _____.

5. _____ is the study of how messages influence people.

6. The term dialectic is the process of using questions and answers to discover or test _____.

7. Informal logic lacks the certainty of _____.

8. The term _____ is the process of using questions and answers to discover or test knowledge.

9. The _____ is a method whereby the two advocates seek the answer to a question by asking a series of questions surrounding the central issue.

10. A(n) _____ is used to support the inference from evidence to claim.

LESSON 2 REVIEW ANSWERS

1. Reasons

2. Argument

3. ability

4. claim

5. Rhetoric

6. knowledge

7. mathematics

8. dialectic

9. Socratic Method

10. warrant

LESSON 3: Reconciliation

Reconciliation as performed in the appraisal process is really reasoning with a critical mind. Of course, *critical mind* means to engage the critical thought process. Reconciliation takes place within the approaches to value and within methods and techniques. In addition, an overall reconciliation takes place at the end of the development portion of the appraisal process and just prior to the reporting portion of an assignment. So, while the term reconciliation is identified at the end of the development stage of the appraisal process, the act of reconciliation is performed throughout the appraisal process.

RECONCILIATION DEFINED

As stated, the reconciliation stage is the final step in the development aspect of the appraisal process. However, reconciliation is not the last step in the appraisal process; reporting or communicating the results is the final step. Think of reconciliation as a process where all that is relevant to the assignment is considered, where opinions and conclusions are formed, where statements are developed and arguments are formed. Reconciliation is a point where everything is tied together, juxtaposed between the development and reporting aspects of the assignment.

Reconciliation means to reach conclusions based on the data uncovered during the assignment. Typically, it is said that an appraiser reconciles at the end of each approach to value and then again at the end of the development aspect of the appraisal process, but this is only partly true.

In fact, there may be other times when an appraisal professional is required to reconcile. For example, reconciliation may be required after highest and best use or during a feasibility analysis. Remember, reconciliation means to reach conclusions based on the data uncovered during the assignment. Therefore, the appraiser must also reconcile all methods and techniques used and their appropriateness. This is important to remember when report writing. The appraiser must reconcile all methods and techniques, must reconcile within the approaches, and also must reconcile to reach logical conclusions using the approaches and data uncovered.

Reconciliation truly is the final step in the development portion of the scientific method, whereby conclusions are made after a summation of the facts uncovered by the results of the study. Sound familiar? The appraisal process begins with a problem, uncovers facts, analyzes this information, and reaches conclusions.

In fact, it can be argued that the scope of work decision, the market analysis process, the highest and best use analysis, the approaches to value, and even the reconciliation process all begin with an issue, have information to analyze, and reach a conclusion after this process of synthesis. These are separate processes, yet they are all interrelated as the information contained within each is predominantly the same. Critical thought is the process that weaves them together. Since the appraisal process depends on each of these subprocesses, it can be said that these processes are contained within an overall process.

In truth, most appraisers are taught that reconciliation takes place in two general areas, within the approaches to value and at the end of the development of an assignment. This answer is fine for a classroom or license exam, but it is not truly accurate. This is why many appraisers lack critical thinking in their assignments. This lack of critical thinking in no way makes for a better appraiser. When one believes that there are only two points of reconciliation (four if you are completing three approaches to value), then the entire point about the scientific method is lost. The process of reconciliation sets up the all-important step of critical thinking, which should be done throughout the appraisal process, from problem identification through reporting.

The Process of Reconciliation

The process of reconciliation is fairly straightforward:

- Consider the relevant facts
- Determine how they match up with the problem or issue
- Reach conclusions based on sound reasoning and critical thinking
- Disclose the reasoning to the reader of the report

Where Are the Errors?

So where does an assignment go wrong? The appraisal process seems to be foolproof, and if the appraisal professional takes time to perform the assignment in a due diligent manner, all should be well, right? Not necessarily. The problem is not always in the performance, but in the lack of critical thinking as a result of either shortcuts or shortcomings.

Most appraisers know to work through the appraisal process; this is not the issue. It is how one performs the process and interprets the data that begs the question of competency. Do you see the appraisal process and, indeed, the processes of scope of work, market analysis, highest and best use, and reporting as separate, unrelated, individual checklists to be performed to reach a conclusion to the assignment? If so, then you are likely missing the point of the processes and the necessary critical thought process for completing more complex highest and best use, feasibility study, and market study analyses is likely to be lacking in your performance of such assignments. What's worse, this viewpoint is likely to reduce one's effectiveness in reporting the results of an assignment even on noncomplex properties.

Remember to take the time to think critically and use your specialized knowledge wisely as a professional; this is what your client is paying you to do. Further, remember that the appraisal process is a two-part process of developing and reporting.

- Developing is the stage where data is gathered, verified, analyzed, and synthesized.

- Reconciliation is where the reasoning takes place to finalize opinions and conclusions.

- Reasoning is the basis of reconciliation and reasoning is the basis of argument.

- Reporting is the stage where your argument is communicated to the intended user of the report for the assignment.

As an appraisal professional, begin with the basics and remain true to them as you evolve professionally and you will be revered as a competent appraisal professional and someone that all appraisers would be proud to call our peer.

LESSON 3 REVIEW QUESTIONS

1. The final step in the development aspect of the appraisal process is known as _____.

2. Reach conclusions based on sound reasoning and _____ thinking.

3. The last step in the appraisal process is _____.

4. Most appraisers are taught that reconciliation takes place in two general areas, within the _____ and _____ of an assignment.

5. And above all, _____ the reasoning to the reader of the report.

6. Most appraisers readily recognize that reconciliation takes place after the approaches to value as well as at the end of the development stage of the appraisal process. But reconciliation should also take place after each recognized _____ and _____.

7. _____ means to reach conclusions based on the data uncovered.

8. Think of reconciliation as a process where all that is _____ to the assignment is considered.

9. Reconciliation is a point where everything is tied together; it is _____ between the development and reporting of the assignment.

10. The appraisal process begins with a problem, uncovers facts, analyzes information, and reaches _____.

LESSON 3 REVIEW ANSWERS

1. reconciliation

2. critical

3. report or communicate the results

4. approaches to value; at the conclusion of development

5. disclose

6. methods; techniques

7. Reconciliation

8. relevant

9. juxtaposed

10. conclusions

SECTION 1 REVIEW QUESTIONS

1. The appraisal process begins with
   a. communicating the results.
   b. reconciling to conclusions.
   c. identifying the problem.
   d. None of the above

2. The performance standards of any profession are strict requirements to ensure proper delivery of _____ assignment results.
   a. confusing
   b. credible
   c. the highest
   d. the lowest

3. Within this first step in the appraisal process, the appraiser must
   a. identify the client and other intended users of the report.
   b. identify the intended use of the report and the appraiser's opinions and conclusions.
   c. identify and locate the real estate.
   d. All of the above

4. Scope of work determination begins with the _____ process.
   a. engagement
   b. billing
   c. reporting
   d. None of the above

5. The scope of work decision is largely dictated by the _____ needs and intended use of the appraisal, along with the assignment conditions.
   a. borrower's
   b. appraiser's
   c. client's
   d. attorney's

6. The five basic functions of management include
   a. plan and organize.
   b. staff, direct, and control.
   c. Both a and b
   d. Neither a nor b

7. Reconciliation is the final step in the _____ aspect of the appraisal process, but communicating the results is the final step in the _____ process.
   a. development; appraisal
   b. appraisal; development
   c. scope of work; data collection
   d. data collection; scope of work

8. _____ thought is part of the appraisal process and a key component of the performance standard for appraisal professionals.
   a. Critical
   b. Crucial
   c. Common
   d. Customary

9. Neglecting to perform critical thought is
   a. incompetence.
   b. okay, under certain circumstances.
   c. sanctioned by *USPAP*.
   d. None of the above

10. Argumentation is the study of effective
    a. writing.
    b. reasoning.
    c. fighting.
    d. debating.

11. _____ is the study of how messages influence people.
    a. Argumentation
    b. Rhetoric
    c. Assent
    d. Communication

12. Reconciliation takes place
    a. within the approaches to value.
    b. within methods and techniques.
    c. Both a and b
    d. occasionally.

13. The process of reconciliation includes
    a. the consideration of relevant facts.
    b. determining how the facts match up with the problem or issue.
    c. reaching conclusions based on sound reasoning and critical thinking.
    d. All of the above

14. Reconciliation
    a. means to reach conclusions based on the data uncovered during the assignment.
    b. is not the last step in the appraisal process.
    c. is a process where all that is relevant to the assignment is considered.
    d. All of the above

15. What are the three criteria for being considered a profession?
    a. Licensing, qualifications, and public trust
    b. Education, licensing, and public trust
    c. Education/qualifications, ethics/standards, and public trust
    d. Licensing, education, and qualifications

16. Public trust can be abused by
    a. the actions of an individual within a profession.
    b. the lack of enforcement within a profession.
    c. Neither a nor b
    d. Both a and b

17. As a practicing professional, my concerns for public trust are extended to
    a. my actions only.
    b. my actions and the actions of my peers.
    c. my actions, the actions of my peers, and the actions of the enforcement agencies of my profession.
    d. None of the above

18. Having a code of ethics and a clearly identified standard under which the professional must practice is known as
    a. the Ethics Provision.
    b. the Standard of Practice.
    c. Appraisal Qualifications.
    d. the Preamble.

REPORT WRITING

LESSON 1: Effective Communication

LESSON 2: Writing: Grammar, Composition, and Essay

LESSON 3: Reporting and the Standards

LEARNING OBJECTIVES

By the end of this section, participants will be able to

- define effective communication;

- be familiar with the various levels of audience expertise;

- understand the significance of audience assessment;

- recognize how to assess an audience;

- understand the strategy for effective communication;

- understand basic grammar;

- recognize the eight parts of speech;

- distinguish between essay and composition; and

- understand the process of essay.

KEY TERMS

audience	data dump	information overload
communication	effective	narrative
communication process	communication	pathos
	essay	verbal illustration
composition	information dump	visual illustration

LESSON 1: Effective Communication

We are, all of us, a summation of every event and every experience in our lives. Each of us has developed moment by moment to the exact person that we are, right here, right now. Our environment, our culture, our education, virtually everyone we have come in contact with has served to shape us into the person we are. Every moment in our lives has an influence upon us, albeit some more profound than others. How we respond to these stimuli is also varied. Ask any parent with more than one child and he will confirm how each child has his or her own personality reflective of this truth. Even twins or triplets who are born within moments of each other and spend most of their childhood a few feet apart are likely to react differently to the same situation. One child sees a clown's face and laughs, while the other is terrified and cries.

Evoking a response from others is the focus of this lesson. Whether we are trying to inform, inquire, request, or persuade, we are using a process called *communication*. Passing information along to someone is one thing, but to gain a desired reaction from someone is quite different.

Communication is another term that society identifies as something that we do all the time, and something so commonplace that it does not need to be formally studied. Many people seem to believe that communication is waiting for someone to finish talking so that "I can begin to speak," or at least that is the way it seems based on their actions.

Similar to passing information versus gaining a response, speaking is one thing and listening is quite another, but communication is not simply putting the two together and hoping for the best. Communication is a skill that must be honed and constantly developed to be truly effective.

Communication is the sharing of knowledge between sender and receiver through messages. To communicate effectively should imply to you that we are speaking of communication with an audience in mind with the intention of having some sort of effect. **Effective communication** is, therefore, the sharing of knowledge with an audience in mind. We will investigate effective communication further, but first let's look at the **communication process**.

FIGURE 2.1
The Communication Process

THE COMMUNICATION PROCESS

Because we come from such varied backgrounds and levels of education, our ability to "communicate" whether we are a sender or receiver of messages is constantly in question. Therefore, there is no way to know precisely how any person will react to what we communicate, or if we have spoken in terms that they can truly understand. We might share a common language and come from similar backgrounds, and yet the words that we use and how we use them might "communicate" an unintended message to the receiver.

In virtually any environment we are constantly bombarded with messages. Verbal, written, visual, audio, tactile, and nonverbal messages are all around us. We send and receive messages in so many forms throughout the day one should think that we would all become very proficient in this skill set early on in life. In truth, communication can break down relatively easily, even in its simplest form. The following is an outline of how communication takes place:

1. The sender must begin with a notion or a thought, which is translated to a message within the sender's mind.

2. The message is transferred to a medium such as a written document, an oral statement, or some other form.

3. The message is delivered to the receiver.

4. The receiver must decipher or translate the message to the best of his or her ability based on the interpretation of the message.

5. If required, a reaction or response is manufactured in the mind of the receiver. (See Figure 2.1.)

While this system seems elementary and oversimplified, we can easily see several places where communication can break down. From the genesis of the sender's thought to the acceptance and acknowledged understanding in the mind of the receiver, much can happen.

The Effective Communication Process

The communication process is quite simple and yet there are several areas of potential pitfalls that can take place within the process. While communication takes place continually in most people's lives throughout the day, effective communication is something altogether different. Effective communication starts with an appeal to a specific audience and ends with a response from the audience that the sender wishes to elicit. There are four steps in effective communication strategy:

1. Establish the objective for your communication

2. Identify the target audience

3. Choose the most effective communication medium for your needs

4. Create and communicate the message

In the case of appraisal report writing, the objective is to transfer the knowledge that has been uncovered in the appraisal process. Further, the report must reach answers, opinions, and conclusions to the question outlined in the problem identification step and gain the assent of the audience. How is this done? Using the four steps of effective communication strategy, consider the following steps in the effective communication process for reporting and appraisal assignment:

1. Establish the objective for your communication
   - Problem identification within the appraisal process
   - Scope of work

2. Identify the target audience
   - Assess the target audience
   - Develop an appeal for the audience

3. Choose the most effective communication medium for your needs
   - Oral report
   - Narrative report
   - Form report

4. Create and communicate the message
   - Choose the content of the message
   - Organize thoughts in the message
   - Write the message
   - Revise, edit, and proofread the message

Effective communication is no different than report writing. In fact, the word *report* can be substituted for the word *message* in the above steps. The balance of this lesson will be spent on considering the audience and the best method of appealing to the audience.

The Audience

As appraisal professionals we have an ethical obligation to draft reports that are not misleading. How then do we ensure that our thoughts are precisely understood and interpreted as we intended? Further, how do we influence or persuade the client or intended user of our report that we are correct in our analysis and opinions? How do we convince the audience that we have fulfilled the burden of proof of supporting our claims with evidence and reason and that we deserve their assent?

We have alluded to the importance of considering the **audience** so that we might more effectively communicate our thoughts. Aristotle understood this phenomenon all too well when he wrote the following passage from *The Rhetoric*:

> . . . persuasion may come through the hearers when the speech stirs their emotions. Our judgments when we are pleased and friendly are not the same as when we are pained and hostile.

You will note that not only does Aristotle identify a need to strike the emotion of the listener, but he also identifies something basic to human nature in that we respond better to words, presentations, and arguments that please us. Now, sometimes it is impossible to please a reader who has discovered through your work that there is a problem or negative issue concerning a property or its value. But in truth, the reader should be pleased with the manner in which the information has been transferred.

The concept of striking the audience's emotion to gain some level of persuasion is what Aristotle referred to as *pathos*. **Pathos** refers to the ability of the speaker to connect with the feelings, wishes, desires, fears, and passions of the audience. We use the Greek derivative of the word *pathos* in our own language with words such as sym*path*y and em*path*y.

In pleasing the audience, we can persuade the reader to find agreement with our argument. How then does one connect with the audience or communicate so that the reader will be pleased? The answer is fairly simple, but consistently overlooked in report writing: keeping the audience in mind throughout the reporting process. Ask questions such as the following:

- What would I want to know about this topic if I were the reader?

- How would I like to be presented with this information?

- Does this information make sense?

- Do the arguments make sense?

- Does the content of this report flow well?

- Have I reached the truth of the matter, and will this have an effect on the reader?

In the words of the great Roman statesman and orator Cicero, "If you wish to persuade me, you must think my thoughts, feel my feelings, and speak my words." This statement is so profoundly true that we must break it down for analysis.

"If you wish to persuade me..."   To persuade anyone of anything requires an appeal to their judgment whereby you are wishing to influence their behavior, attitude, or thoughts. In the context of appraisal report writing you are attempting to gain the assent of the reader toward your argument, to persuade the reader into adherence with your opinions and conclusions using solid evidence and reasoning.

Very well, we understand the goal, but how do we accomplish this goal? It seems that Cicero has provided us the answer to this question as well.

"...you must think my thoughts..."   One cannot be more absolute than using the word *must*. We must think like the audience. Understand what the audience is hoping to discover from your report. Ask yourself the obvious questions, What does my audience want to know? Why have my services been engaged?

It is vital that we develop our persuasive arguments from the critical reader's perspective. Keep in mind that the assumption here is that the critical reader is to be the client and the intended user. We shall see in the next lesson that the style of most people's writing is for "a reader, any reader." But when we refer to the critical reader, our intention is to emphasize the knowledgeable reader for whom the report is intended to be drafted and read. The critical reader, like the critical listener in argumentation, is someone that will apply the critical thought process to our claims, opinions, and conclusions.

"...you must feel my feelings..."   To feel someone's feelings is akin to empathizing with them, to being able to relate to their needs and wants. Note the word *empathize* includes the Greek root *pathos*. This is also vital to gaining the assent of the audience because no reaction is possible without some sort of emotional connection. Albeit, the connection here is on a very primitive and almost subconscious level.

It must resonate with the audience that you truly understand the issues and that you understand and have identified with their needs. This is a very powerful thing! You cannot fake this part of the equation. Your writing must reflect that you have given thought to the situation, that you recognize the important issues at hand, and that you understand how the issues affect the reader's concerns.

There is no substitute for the truth, and that is what you must emphasize within your report. This is what we mean when we refer to maintaining credibility throughout the process. We are not saying that we are committing ourselves to communicate a "touchy-feely" approach to reporting—not at all. We are saying that no matter how our opinions and conclusions affect the reader, our job is to be truthful and professional. As such, our attempts to gain the reader's agreement are based on sound argument and logical connections to the truth of the matter. This should be received with the same professional and informative spirit in which it is being projected.

After considering the claims made and the opinions presented along with the evidence that has been provided, the critical reader should either accept the resolution or reject the argument and shift the presumption by providing other evidence in support of another viewpoint that supports that shift. In other words, the critical reader should accept the supported argument or challenge the argument with evidence that provides for a different conclusion. Once a supported claim is made, it is not appropriate for the critical reader to simply disagree because he or she does not like the results.

The reader might not like the answer, but the point is that it is the true answer to this problem. Further, the presumption should be that the writer has developed the assignment results in a manner that is according to the standard of practice using recognized methods and techniques and relevant information that has been verified. If this is not shown to be the case, then the case itself should be rejected, and it is well within the rights of the critical reader to demand more explanation, evidence, support, and so on.

"...you must speak my words." This point simply means to talk to me in a language that I understand. Do not use confusing words, acronyms, jargon, or incomplete thoughts in your description of the case. Be direct and clear by choosing words that are not ambiguous! Your words should be accurate and not be subject to multiple interpretations.

While your explanations might seem simple enough to you, they might be a bit lofty for the reader. Report writers almost always overestimate the level of understanding of their clients. One reason is that our terminology, methods, techniques, technology, and services have become so commonplace and familiar to us that they seem easy to understand. We see this particularly in consulting assignments where the client knows what is needed from the appraiser, yet the client is unfamiliar with the nuances of valuation methods, principles, and techniques. Of course, the appraisal professional will make the mistake of assuming that the client is far more versed in all aspects of valuation because of the level of intelligence shown in engaging the assignment.

Clients will seldom tell us that they don't understand something because there is an intimidation factor that forces the client to think, "Should I know this? I should know this, right? Why don't I know this? Well, I'll just proceed as if I know this." And the sad part of it all is that you have missed an opportunity to become more valuable to your client by providing explanations.

How does one avoid this? Evaluate the reader and the reader's experience level and remain consciously aware of your reader. If you are writing for multiple audiences with varying experience levels, then you must write for the least knowledgeable first. Consider the following four audience and the expertise possibilities:

1. The uninformed audience

2. The acquainted audience

3. The informed audience

4. The expert audience

Let's look at how our writing should appeal to each level of expertise.

The Uninformed Audience

An uninformed audience does not mean generally ignorant or uneducated, it means uninformed about what appraisers do! The great American folk comedian Will Rogers used to say, "Everyone is ignorant, just on different stuff."

This point is well stated when speaking of the uninformed audience. It could be that your reader is an Ivy League–educated CEO of a major corporation and just does not understand the appraisal process or some of the routine methods and techniques that are used in valuation.

A reader in this audience is likely to be a one-time user of your services. The uniformed audience is likely to be someone that carefully reads your cover letter (letter of transmittal), skims through the rest of the report for content, and then reads with care the areas of analysis or conclusions, such as the sections containing reconciliation. Further, the uniformed reader is looking for graphics or other visuals to help explain the information in a manner that is more understandable. The details and technical information will be left for a colleague or employee with experience in those areas to critique. Here are some suggestions for writing for the uninformed reader:

■ Keep the cover letter short, businesslike, and to the point with precise accuracy. Avoid words or terms that require explanation such as acronyms or specialized definitions. Sometimes definitions are unavoidable, as when you are performing an analysis that requires a hypothetical condition or an extraordinary assumption (see current edition of *USPAP*).

In such cases a definition should be provided that is precise and quoted directly from the source.

- Keep your focus from the opening sentence and throughout the report on the specific functionality that will allow the reader to understand the report. This way, if the material requires specialized knowledge or a higher level of expertise to interpret, the reader can scan past or ask for clarity from a more knowledgeable colleague or some other similar source.

- Do not confuse the reader with too much information, especially that of a technical nature. This subjects a reader to *information overload*. **Information overload** is when the reader becomes confused because there is too much information, particularly when the information is specialized. Provide only the information that the reader needs.

- Keep the writing very basic. Short is better than long, simple is better than complex. Focus the attention on what this means to the reader, rather than how this works.

- Use illustrations and keep them simple. There are two main methods of illustration: *visual illustration* and *verbal illustration*. **Visual illustrations** are graphs, maps, photos, outlines, and charts. **Verbal illustrations** are famous quotes, metaphors, anecdotes, comparisons, and analogies. By making your point concrete and equating it to something that everyone can understand you have moved closer to connecting with the audience.

- Avoid using industry jargon. Jargon makes the reader feel like an outsider, and that is intimidating. Have you ever talked to an IT guy about your AV or why the CRT is not working on your PC? We have our own acronyms such as *USPAP (Uniform Standards of Professional Appraisal Practice)* and GFWA (gas forced warm air) to name a couple. If you must use them, at least define the acronym the first time you use it before repeating it throughout your writing.

- Avoid referencing resources that are commonly used in appraising. This reader will not use such resources and will not likely have access to them. If you must refer to information taken from such resources, provide a copy in an appendix section of the report.

- Describe all procedures or processes in an easy step-by-step manner. Allow the reader to understand how the processes work and what is significant about the results.

- Highlight your main points and make all transitions obvious. Reinforce your messages with typography, borders, boldface, color, and anything else that makes the main points jump off the page.

The Acquainted Audience

A reader in the acquainted audience category is likely to be someone who reads appraisals often. This audience is acquainted with your profession, is aware of what should be included in the report, and will likely be more responsive to your opinions, recommendations, and conclusions. But with this higher level of understanding comes a greater level of critical analysis on the part of the reader. Most typical users of appraisal services fall into this category. The acquainted audience understands methods and techniques, but might not understand the appropriateness of using them.

All of the guidelines for the uninformed audience are appropriate for the acquainted audience with some additional liberties allowed. Some general jargon and familiar acronyms are acceptable, but as with the uniformed audience, these should be defined the first time they are used. Some suggestions for writing for the acquainted audience are as follows:

- More complex graphics are acceptable at this level provided that they are clear and accurate.

- Generally known terms or jargon can be used, but in a context that makes it easy to discern their meaning.

- Resources should be accessible to this level, otherwise the information should be provided in an appendix, not simply referenced.

The Informed Audience

The informed audience has extensive knowledge of your field, although they might not expressly practice as an appraisal professional. Many underwriters fall into this category. The reader in this audience is looking for anything that establishes links between what is familiar to what is new. While the reader in this category has specialized knowledge of your field, there might be a lack of understanding in complex cases or events that are outside the norm. Most of your reports are critiqued by the informed reader. Some suggestions for writing for the informed audience are as follows:

- Highlight those issues that are beyond the norm. This reader is so familiar with the norm that anything that falls outside of the norm will be found out and scrutinized. Better to gain the confidence of this reader by being up-front with peculiar issues or concerns.

- Create technically sound reports using recognized methods and techniques.

- Use appropriate methods and techniques when writing the report as this reader is good at recognizing flimsy arguments and usually understands the appropriateness of the methods and techniques used.

- Stay focused and centered, keeping transitions in thought logical and rational.

- Avoid including irrelevant information. This reader will reject data dump or information dump. **Data dump** and **information dump** are slang terms for either including too much irrelevant information in your writing or including information without analysis. In report writing this is called "fluff" and it is a mechanism of poor report writing. What's worse, fluff is easy to spot and implies that the writer has nothing important to say. Give this reader too much irrelevant information or data without analysis and your report will immediately lose credibility.

The Expert Audience

A reader in the expert audience knows as much about your field as you do. The expert is likely to be an appraiser, and would also likely qualify as an appraisal peer. An appraiser's peer is an appraiser that has expertise and competency in a similar type of assignment. An expert audience not only has an extensive knowledge of your field, but also has detailed knowledge and familiarity with the latest methods, techniques, resources, and applications. An expert audience is well-versed in the appropriateness of the information, methods, and techniques presented in the report. The guidelines noted for the acquainted reader are all in force with the expert reader with some additional cautions. Additional guidelines when writing for the expert audience are as follows:

- The use of jargon and acronyms are more acceptable for this reader but be judicious. Even an expert's eyes will gloss over with the use of too much insider language or too many acronyms.

- Provide technical background in a manner that is not too elementary.

- Keep details of math, equations, statistics, and other technical information in the body of the report and in areas where they are expected to be placed.

- Maintain your objectivity and use a professional tone. Be familiar, but do not slip into casual familiarity with the reader. You are, after all, making an argument for your opinions and conclusions.

Once the level of expertise of the audience is properly assessed, the appeal to the audience can begin with precision. Knowing the audience is only the beginning to knowing the best way to speak to audience. The most effective communicators are those that strike the emotion, address the important issues, support all claims with evidence, and argue on relevant grounds.

Remember, the audience is a critical reader. Ensuring that the message is understood is undoubtedly the most crucial concern of a report writer. Sometimes a form report is adequate to transfer information, other times the situation is simply not addressed with a checked box on a form. The great American general George S. Patton once said, "Fixed fortifications are monuments to the stupidity of men." While the good general was speaking about military installations such as forts or ramparts, his point works well with respect to report writing. If you allow a form to dictate what you are allowed to say then you might find yourself in trouble when you are faced with a need to say more. Never let a form or time limit what you absolutely have an obligation to report.

Effective communication also means that you have truthfully and accurately covered the relevant issues of the case. In form reporting, if there is not enough room for the explanation that is required, then an addendum is needed. Be sure to recount throughout the report that there is an attached addendum. Sometimes such documents might be mysteriously removed from the report, especially if the information contained within the addendum is less than desirable for the client to have in the file. Hey, it happens!

The point here is that you are the captain of your ship, which means that you have a responsibility to report credible results in a manner that is *not* misleading. Sometimes the information can easily be transferred in a form report, and other times a narrative report is required.

In effective communication the term **narrative** means something akin to story telling. The point about narrative is well captured in the following passage:

The Importance of "Narrative"

Everyone loves a good story! Hollywood has built a multi-billion-dollar empire upon good stories. Indeed, some of America's greatest speakers have been proficient storytellers. Mark Twain, Will Rogers, and Ernest Hemingway were all great narrators. Something about the way they wrote rivets us to their words, and the sound of their written voice soothes us. But is that what endears them to us, or is it something more? Is it something that is unspoken yet ever-present? The sense of immortal writing carries with it an almost simplistic quality that allows the masses to identify with the piece. This symbiotic relationship between story teller and listener is what elevates the writer to immortal status. What reader cannot identify with the simple Mississippi River charm of Twain's characters? Who has not felt the pain Hemingway describes as the embattled old man struggles with his enormous catch? And when Will Rogers says, "You know, I just don't understand politicians," well, what CEO or dock worker can't identify with that statement? Their words bring us to a commonality that transcends all levels of intellect, education, or professional status. Their words speak to the human condition with which we all can identify.

Narration will always be the best way to identify with people, and vice versa. Narration helps to explain the details of our case in a manner that is clear and logical. We are curious creatures and we all love a good story, just keep it informative and interesting!

The point of the above passage is to show that sometimes the best way to say something is to just say it. While it is likely possible to set a matrix of boxes to check that would describe the important points of the passage, this does not allow for a connection between writer and reader. Narratives should be used whenever possible, particularly when extraordinary issues require explanation.

Sometimes the use of narrative is not recommended and a visual illustration is more appropriate. Of the following two formats, which would you rather read?

■ **In Practice**

Capitalization Method and Rate

The loan to value ratio is based on a 70/30 with an annual interest rate of 7 percent and a rate to the equity of 9 percent. The amortization term is 20 years with a 3- to 5-year balloon. The calculated annual loan constant is therefore set at 0.093036. The mortgage component is calculated at 0.065125 and the equity component is 0.027000 for an overall capitalization rate of 9.3 percent using the band of investments method.

Or

Capitalization Method and Rate

The salient factors which have applied to the subject are shown below:

Ratio of Loan to Value:	70 percent
Equity Ratio:	30 percent
Equity Requirement:	9 percent
Interest Rate:	7 percent
Amortization:	20-year term
Balloon:	3 to 5 years
Annual Constant:	0.093036

Calculation of Overall Rate

$0.70 \times 0.093036 =$	0.065125
$0.30 \times 0.090000 =$	<u>0.027000</u>
	0.093125

Weighted Average (Basic Rate) 0.093125 percent, as rounded 9.3 percent

Overall Rate   9.3 percent

The answer should be quite obvious. While there will always be a delicate balance between what the reader needs to know and how to present the information to the reader, a good rule of thumb is to use your own judgment and ask the fundamental question:

"How would I like to have to read this report?"

LESSON 1 REVIEW QUESTIONS

1. _____ illustrations are famous quotes, metaphors, anecdotes, comparisons, and analogies.

2. Effective communication starts with an appeal to a specific _____.

3. _____ dump or _____ dump are slang terms for either including too much irrelevant information in your writing or including information without analysis.

4. To persuade this reader you must stay focused and centered, keeping the transitions in thought _____ and rational.

5. Keep details of math, equations, statistics, and other technical information in the body of the report and in areas where they are _____ to be placed.

6. The narration will always be the best way to _____ with people and vice versa.

7. In effective communication the term _____ means something akin to story telling.

8. An appraiser's peer is an appraiser that has expertise and _____ in a similar type of assignment.

9. Do not confuse the reader with too much information, especially that of a(n) _____ nature.

10. _____ is when the reader becomes confused because there is too much information, particularly when the information is specialized.

LESSON 1 REVIEW ANSWERS

1. Verbal

2. audience

3. Data; information

4. logical

5. expected

6. identify

7. narrative

8. competency

9. technical

10. Information overload

LESSON 2: Writing: Grammar, Composition, and Essay

WHAT IS GRAMMAR?

Grammar is the systematic rules of a language. In particular, English grammar has terms that provide for a common language when talking about writing. We will review many of these terms, but keep in mind that this course is limited in duration. Further, as drafters of appraisal reports, we are concerned with business writing. This means that basic grammar and composition is our primary concern and that is all we really can comfortably cover within this course. We suggest that you continue to develop your writing skills by attending a more advanced course in composition. This will only strengthen your writing skills, and that is a very good thing!

Knowing the rules of English grammar does not guarantee that you will become a good writer or a great communicator, but it will help you avoid bad writing or unintended communications. Grammar helps the message sender communicate thoughts in a clear and concise manner. Report writing in particular should be as clear and concise as possible. Wordiness or mistakes in grammar are the prime causes of communications that are unclear or misleading. And we know that an appraisal professional cannot afford to be misleading—this leads to a loss of credibility with your audience, and perhaps lawsuits.

Your thoughts and arguments are separate from your delivery. This was Plato's point about the Sophists. A good appraisal professional has honed both skills well. If you don't believe that grammar and writing skills are all that important, consider this: You might have an important point or fascinating opinions and conclusions reflecting perception and insight beyond anyone else, but if your communication contains errors, your audience will likely question what you have said, simply because of the way you have said it. Delivery is as important as the message. A poor delivery yields unintended interpretations by the receiver with costly consequences to the sender. Convinced? Good. Let's proceed.

THE PARTS OF SPEECH

If you want to improve your grammar so that you can write and communicate well, you need to understand the mechanics of sentence structure.

English words are classified into eight parts of speech based on their function within a phrase, clause, or sentence. The parts of speech are noun, verb, adjective, pronoun, adverb, preposition, conjunction, and interjection. Some words have more than one use and therefore more than one classification. A dictionary will provide the abbreviation of the part of speech in context with each definition.

Nouns

A *noun* names a person, place, or thing. A noun can be concrete (truck, house, or dog) or it can be abstract (love, joy, or happiness). Sometimes a word might look like a verb but function as a noun. For example: "*Fishing* is a relaxing sport." The word *fishing* is the name of an activity rather than an action.

Proper nouns are always capitalized, and they name a specific person, place, group, or event. For example: Abraham Lincoln, Mount Rushmore, or the Great Depression. Be careful when capitalizing. Too often words that are not proper nouns are inappropriately capitalized.

Verbs

The *verb* conveys action that is performed by the subject, links the subject to a *complement*, or expresses a state of that subject. Verbs reflect movement or connect the subject in some way.

> "The deer *leaped* high into the air.": *leaped* expresses action.

> "Bob *is* happy.": *is* connects the noun (Bob) to the complement (happy).

We could spend more than the time allotted for this course considering the various types of verbs alone (active voice, inactive voice, transitive, intransitive, gerunds, infinitives, participles, and tenses).

The purpose of this section is to break down proper writing, particularly business writing. A simple reminder of basic sentence structure is all that we are after here.

Nouns and Verbs Together

Nouns and verbs form the basic core of a sentence, and keeping the *agreement* between the two should be the first priority in proper sentence structure. Agreement is an important concept in grammar and, unfortunately, the source of many writing errors. Verbs must agree with their nouns. This means that if the noun is singular, then the verb should also be singular. Of course you will remember that a noun ending in –s is generally plural while a verb ending in –s is usually singular.

> "The cat cries at night." (singular)

> "The cats cry at night." (plural)

Pronouns

A *pronoun* is a word that stands in for a noun. Without pronouns we would simply have to repeat the noun, which is really awkward and redundant!

"John left John's office, taking John's daughter to the theater with John."

"John left his office, taking his daughter to the theater with him."

Like verbs, pronouns are an extensive subject; far too extensive to cover in this course. Also, like nouns and verbs, the first priority of a pronoun is to maintain agreement with the subject. In this case the pronouns *his* and *him* are both singular pronouns matching the singular subject *John*.

Adjectives

An *adjective* modifies a noun or pronoun. A *modifier* describes or limits another word or group of words.

"The *blue* door was attached to the *small* house."

- *Blue* is an adjective modifying door.
- *Small* is an adjective modifying house.

Adverbs

An *adverb* modifies a verb, adjective, or another adverb.

"She laughed *loudly*."

- *Loudly* is an adverb modifying the verb laughed.

"The *very* old man fought off his assailant."

- *Very* is an adverb modifying the adjective old.

"The boy ran *remarkably* fast."

- *Remarkably* is an adverb modifying the adverb fast.

SENTENCES

To move from the parts of speech to sentences is akin to moving from building materials to the building. The infrastructure of a sentence is basic to the structure of conversation. Understanding how sentences are built will help you recognize when a sentence is incomplete, lacks agreement, has misplaced modifiers, or has faulty parallel structure.

A sentence has two parts: a *subject* and a *predicate*. The *subject* is what or whom the sentence is about and the *predicate* tells what the subject does or is, or what is done to the subject. A *simple subject* is a noun or pronoun and a *simple predicate* consists of a verb or an adverb. The *complete subject* is the noun or pronoun and the words that modify the subject. A *complete predicate* is a verb or verb phrase and the words that modify or complete the predicate.

"Julie kissed Tom."

Julie is both the simple and complete subject, while *kissed* is the simple predicate and *kissed Tom* is the complete predicate: the verb *kissed* and its direct object *Tom.*

Complete Thoughts and Context

A sentence should have a complete thought. The following sentence is technically correct and grammatically complete.

"Bill yelled."

The previous sentence is complete, but very boring. There are many questions that we would like to know. Why did Bill yell? What did Bill yell? To whom did Bill yell? These are just a few questions to ask about Bill yelling. The sentence lacks context. Effect communication should always consider whether the reader will understand the context of the sentence. In the above sentence the reader is likely to say, "So Billed yelled. . .what about it?"

Composition

Composition is placing thoughts together to formulate a full message. In writing, thoughts are contained within the sentence and a series of thoughts should be contained within a paragraph. In turn, the paragraph is a group of related sentences. Sentences should flow from one to another and paragraphs should do the same.

ESSAY

Essay is the process of writing a completed message or series of messages. The concern in an essay should be for the reader to easily identify the information. The following is the process for creating an effective essay:

1. Determine the topic

2. Gather relevant information about the topic

3. Formulate a thesis or main idea and decide what points to make

4. Decide on the order in which the points will be placed

5. Write a first draft

6. Edit and revise for content, clarity, and style

7. Write final draft

Determine the Topic and Gather Relevant Information

The assignment already has a topic, and the information required to complete the assignment will be gathered during the appraisal process. However, writing the information in a manner that the critical reader will understand and agree with is another matter all together.

The ideas and the strategy for relaying them to the reader should be determined during the development stage of the assignment. Your overall (or final) reconciliation is likely to direct your strategy for relaying this information to the reader.

Formulate a Thesis or Main Idea and Decide What Points to Make

The main ideas and supporting information should be outlined well in advance of writing the report. To get these ideas in an outline, they must first be grouped and then placed with subtopics. This is where the writer should assess the audience and determine the best way to present the material. The language to be used, the level of knowledge, and the speed at which the information is to be presented should be determined here.

Decide On the Order in Which the Points Will Be Placed

Once you have identified the audience and the main points to be made, along with the level on which you will present the material, determine the proper order of delivery from start to finish.

Write a First Draft

When writing the first draft, concentrate primarily on content and not necessarily correctness. Getting the important ideas on paper in a logical sequence that the audience can follow should be the primary focus here.

Edit and Revise for Content, Clarity, and Style

The following is a list of questions that the writer should ask about the material as a means of completing an edit.

Structural Revision

- What is your purpose, and is it evident in your writing?
- How does each paragraph in your writing support your thesis, and are these relationships clear?
- What details, reasons, or examples have you used to support each of your ideas?
- Do any of your claims, opinions, or conclusions require further support?
- Does the order of your presentation work well?
- Have you drawn relationships among the elements within your argument?

- How does each sentence within the paragraph help develop the context of the paragraph?

- Are the paragraphs unified, coherent, well developed, and complete?

- How effective are your opening and closing paragraphs?

- Are your assertions believable and supportable?

- Is your reasoning rational, are there any faulty areas?

- Are your sentences effective, and do they reach the audience?

- Are your word choices correct?

Proofreading

- Are your sentences grammatically correct?

- Are your sentences clear?

- Is your punctuation correct?

- Spelling?

Write Final Draft   Once all changes have been made, proofread the report yourself first, then have someone else proofread the report. If you can find someone who will enjoy pointing out your mistakes, that is even better.

LESSON 2 REVIEW QUESTIONS

1. The infrastructure of a sentence is basic to the structure of _____.

2. Grammar is the systematic rules of a(n) _____.

3. Knowing the rules of English grammar does not guarantee that you will become a good writer or a great _____.

4. Your thoughts and arguments are separate from your _____.

5. Composition is placing thoughts together to formulate a full _____.

6. The _____ is what or whom the sentence is about.

7. Delivery is as important as the _____.

8. _____ helps the message sender communicate thoughts in a clear and concise manner.

9. A sentence has two parts: a subject and a(n) _____.

10. In report reporting, an appraisal professional cannot afford to be _____.

LESSON 2 REVIEW ANSWERS

1. conversation

2. language

3. communicator

4. delivery

5. message

6. subject

7. message

8. Grammar

9. predicate

10. misleading

LESSON 3: Reporting and the Standards

Standard 2 within the *Uniform Standards of Professional Appraisal Practice* is concerned with the reporting aspect of the appraisal process. Whether it is a written or oral communication of a real property appraisal, Standard 2 reflects the details of the appraiser's responsibility under reporting in a real property appraisal assignment.

Because Standard 2 is concerned with reporting a real property appraisal, it is very similar to Standard 5 (*reporting* an appraisal consulting assignment), Standard 8 (*reporting* a personal property appraisal), Standard 10 (*reporting* a business appraisal), as well as the Standards Rules found in the back part of Standard 3 (developing and *reporting* an appraisal review assignment) and the back part of Standard 6 (developing and *reporting* a mass appraisal assignment).

Standard 2 does not dictate the form, style, or format of real property appraisal reports, but does address the content and level of information required in a real property appraisal report in order to maintain credibility (see advisory opinions AO-16 and AO-26 of *USPAP*). Note that the way a report will be judged is based on the end result. This is what is meant by "The substantive content of a report determines compliance."

STANDARD 2: REAL PROPERTY APPRAISAL, REPORTING

In reporting the results of a real property appraisal, an appraiser must communicate each analysis, opinion, and conclusion in a manner that is not misleading.

Comment: STANDARD 2 addresses the content and level of information required in a report that communicates the results of a real property appraisal.

STANDARD 2 does not dictate the form, format, or style of real property appraisal reports. The form, format, and style of a report are functions of the needs of intended users and appraisers. The substantive content of a report determines its compliance.

■ In Practice

An appraiser conducts an assignment and drafts a report for mortgage consideration. The report reaches a value conclusion and does a very good job of describing how the opinions and value conclusions were reached using the approaches to value, an analysis of the neighborhood, recognized methods and techniques, and so on.

The appraiser neither discussed nor mentioned the implications of a recently approved prospective development containing several similar properties to the subject. The project that is about to be constructed would clearly compete with the subject's marketability should it be placed on the market during the absorption period of this new project.

The bank client in this case phones the appraiser and is very upset that he didn't learn about the new development until after the loan was approved. The client further states that "this loan would never have been approved if you had told us about the project that is coming online."

Is there a violation of Standard 2 in reporting?

Solution

Yes. The appraiser has clearly not met the expectations of the client. The term "for mortgage consideration" is a broad term and needs to be defined during the engagement process of the assignment. While the appraiser cannot be expected to know the lending criteria of the bank-client in this case, there is an obligation to meet the expectations of the client. The standard of practice further requires an analysis of all relevant information pertinent to the assignment, particularly if there are value implications indicated by the information.

The appraiser might claim that the competing project was taken into consideration when the value conclusion was reached, but then the question becomes, "Where is this stated within the report?"

If, like most appraisals drafted for mortgage purposes, the assignment was to determine market value, then market value is to be fixed to a market-derived exposure time, which should have been discussed within the appraisal report. [See *USPAP* Standards Rule 1-2 (c) (iv).] If the market value conclusion reached took into consideration the effects of the new project and it was determined to have had no effect, then the project and its noneffect should have been mentioned.

If the project was determined to have had an effect that is reflected in the value, then any effect on the value and how the conclusions were affected should have been mentioned within the report. Since market changes are readily identifiable, whether they will have an effect on value or not, then the changes should have been reported.

Standards Rule 2-1 (c) reiterates the not misleading aspect of public trust. Further, Standards Rule 2-1 requires the appraiser to "clearly and accurately disclose all assumptions, extraordinary assumptions, hypothetical conditions, and limiting conditions."

Standards Rule 2-1

Each written or oral real property appraisal report must:

(a)   **clearly and accurately set forth the appraisal in a manner that will not be misleading;**

(b)   **contain sufficient information to enable the intended users of the appraisal to understand the report properly; and**

(c)   **clearly and accurately disclose all assumptions, extraordinary assumptions, hypothetical conditions, and limiting conditions used in the assignment.**

Standards Rule 2-2 discusses the appraiser's responsibility to supply a report that contains sufficient information for the intended user to understand it properly.

The reporting characteristics of a written report are also discussed. The three reporting options are outlined and, it should be noted, the persons expected to use a self-contained or summary report may include parties other than the client, while only the client is expected to use a restricted use report (see also AO-12, *Use of the Appraisal Report Options*).

Standards Rule 2-2

Each written real property appraisal report must be prepared under one of the following three options and prominently state which option is used: Self-Contained Appraisal Report, Summary Appraisal Report, or Restricted Use Appraisal Report.[16]

Comment: When the intended users include parties other than the client, either a Self-Contained Appraisal Report or a Summary Appraisal Report must be provided. When the intended users do not include parties other than the client, a Restricted Use Appraisal Report may be provided.

The essential difference among these three options is in the content and level of information provided. The appropriate reporting option and the level of information necessary in the report are dependent on the intended use and the intended users.

An appraiser must use care when characterizing the type of report and level of information communicated upon completion of an assignment. An appraiser may use any other label in addition to, but not in place of, the label set forth in this Standard for the type of report provided.

The report content and level of information requirements set forth in this Standard are minimums for each type of report. An appraiser must supplement a report form, when necessary, to ensure that any intended user of the appraisal is not misled and that the report complies with the applicable content requirements set forth in this Standards Rule.

---

[16] See Advisory Opinion 11, *Content of the Appraisal Report Options of Standards Rules 2-2 and 8-2*, and Advisory Opinion 12, *Use of the Appraisal Report Options of Standards Rules 2-2 and 8-2*. References to Advisory Opinions are for guidance only and do not incorporate Advisory Opinions into USPAP.

The appraiser is the one who identifies the intended user of an appraisal report. Because the intended use drives the information required and, therefore, the applicability of report, the appraiser must match the report with the use. A self-contained report describes the information analyzed, while a summary report summarizes the information analyzed and a restricted use report simply states the information. The level of detail is the primary difference between the reporting options. However, the appraiser's work file *must* contain information sufficient to produce, at the very least, a summary report.

A party receiving a copy of a Self-Contained Appraisal Report, Summary Appraisal Report, or Restricted Use Appraisal Report in order to satisfy disclosure requirements does not become an intended user of the appraisal unless the appraiser identifies such party as an intended user as part of the assignment.

The essential difference between Standards Rules 2-2(a), 2-2(b), and 2-2(c) is the level of detail between a self-contained, summary, and restricted use report (see AO-11, *Content of the Appraisal Report Options*).

(a) **The content of a Self-Contained Appraisal Report must be consistent with the intended use of the appraisal and, at a minimum:**

(i) **state the identity of the client and any intended users, by name or type;[17]**

Comment: An appraiser must use care when identifying the client to ensure a clear understanding and to avoid violations of the Confidentiality section of the ETHICS RULE. In those rare instances when the client wishes to remain anonymous, an appraiser must still document the identity of the client in the workfile but may omit the client's identity in the report.

In engaging a client through an attorney, an appraiser must expressly notify each party how the client status and intended user status work in this situation. (See Statement 9, and AO-25, AO-26, and AO-27.)

Intended users of the report might include parties such as lenders, employees of government agencies, partners of a client, and a client's attorney and accountant.

(ii) **state the intended use of the appraisal;[18]**

(iii) **describe information sufficient to identify the real estate involved in the appraisal, including the physical and economic property characteristics relevant to the assignment;[19]**

Comment: The real estate involved in the appraisal can be specified, for example, by a legal description, address, map reference, copy of a survey or map, property sketch and/or photographs or the like. The information can include a property sketch and photographs in addition to written comments about the legal, physical, and economic attributes of the real estate relevant to the type and definition of value and intended use of the appraisal.

The property rights appraised must be expressly stated within the report.

(iv)   **state the real property interest appraised;**

<u>Comment</u>: The statement of the real property rights being appraised must be substantiated, as needed, by copies or summaries of title descriptions or other documents that set forth any known encumbrances.

The appraiser *must* cite the definition of value being sought, and also *must* cite the source of the definition. It is also required to clearly indicate to the intended user(s) how the definition is being applied.

(v)   **state the type and definition of value and cite the source of the definition;**

<u>Comment</u>: Stating the definition of value also requires any comments needed to clearly indicate to intended users how the definition is being applied.[20]

When reporting an opinion of market value, state whether the opinion of value is:
- in terms of cash or of financing terms equivalent to cash, or
- based on non-market financing or financing with unusual conditions or incentives.

When an opinion of market value is not in terms of cash or based on financing terms equivalent to cash, summarize the terms of such financing and explain their contributions to or negative influence on value.

The date of report is usually the date of transmittal letter. Either way, the appraiser *must* make the distinction between the reporting date and the effective date. See the following:

(vi)   **state the effective date of the appraisal and the date of the report;[21]**

<u>Comment</u>: The effective date of the appraisal establishes the context for the value opinion, while the date of the report indicates whether the perspective of the appraiser on the market or property use conditions as of the effective date of the appraisal was prospective, current, or retrospective.

Remember that the scope of work decision must match the clients needs and intended use of the report, and that the burden of proof for making the scope of work decision is on the appraiser.

(vii)   **describe the scope of work used to develop the appraisal;[22]**

> <u>Comment</u>: Because intended users' reliance on an appraisal may be affected by the scope of work, the report must enable them to be properly informed and not misled. Sufficient information includes disclosure of research and analyses performed and might also include disclosure of research and analyses not performed.

> If significant assistance is given by another individual, the appraiser *must* disclose such assistance.

> When any portion of the work involves significant real property appraisal assistance, the appraiser must describe the extent of that assistance. The signing appraiser must also state the name(s) of those providing the significant real property appraisal assistance in the certification, in accordance with SR 2-3.

(viii)   **describe the information analyzed, the appraisal methods and techniques employed, and the reasoning that supports the analyses, opinions, and conclusions; exclusion of the sales comparison approach, cost approach, or income approach must be explained;**

> <u>Comment</u>: A Self-Contained Appraisal Report must include sufficient information to indicate that the appraiser complied with the requirements of STANDARD 1. The amount of detail required will vary with the significance of the information to the appraisal.

> The appraiser must provide sufficient information to enable the client and intended users to understand the rationale for the opinions and conclusions, including reconciliation of the data and approaches, in accordance with Standards Rule 1-6.

> As stated, in a market value appraisal all sales, options, and listings should be uncovered in the normal course of business and analyzed and summarized.

> When reporting an opinion of market value, a summary of the results of analyzing the subject sales, options, and listings in accordance with Standards Rule 1-5 is required. If such information is unobtainable, a statement on the efforts undertaken by the appraiser to obtain the information is required. If such information is irrelevant, a statement acknowledging the existence of the information and citing its lack of relevance is required.

(ix)   **state the use of the real estate existing as of the date of value and the use of the real estate reflected in the appraisal; and, when an opinion of highest and best use was developed by the appraiser, describe the support and rationale for that opinion;**

> See hypothetical conditions and extraordinary assumptions in the Definitions section of *USPAP*.

(x)   **clearly and conspicuously:**

- **state all extraordinary assumptions and hypothetical conditions; and**
- **state that their use might have affected the assignment results; and**

Comment: The report must contain the appraiser's opinion as to the highest and best use of the real estate, unless an opinion as to highest and best use is unnecessary, such as in insurance valuation or value in use appraisals. When reporting an opinion of market value, the appraisers support and rationale for the opinion of highest and best use is required. The appraiser's reasoning in support of the opinion must be provided in the depth and detail required by its significance to the appraisal.

(xi)   **include a signed certification in accordance with Standards Rule 2-3.**

(b)   **The content of a Summary Appraisal Report must be consistent with the intended use of the appraisal and, at a minimum:**

Comment: The essential difference between the Self-Contained Appraisal Report and the Summary Appraisal Report is the level of detail of presentation.

(i)   **state the identity of the client and any intended users, by name or type;[23]**

Comment: An appraiser must use care when identifying the client to ensure a clear understanding and to avoid violations of the Confidentiality section of the ETHICS RULE. In those rare instances when the client wishes to remain anonymous, an appraiser must still document the identity of the client in the workfile but may omit the client's identity in the report.

Intended users of the report might include parties such as lenders, employees of government agencies, partners of a client, and a client's attorney and accountant.

(ii)   **state the intended use of the appraisal;[24]**

(iii)   **summarize information sufficient to identify the real estate involved in the appraisal, including the physical and economic property characteristics relevant to the assignment;[25]**

Comment: The real estate involved in the appraisal can be specified, for example, by a legal description, address, map reference, copy of a survey or map, property sketch, and/or photographs or the like. The summarized information can include a property sketch and photographs in addition to written comments about the legal, physical, and economic attributes of the real estate relevant to the type and definition of value and intended use of the appraisal.

(iv)   **state the real property interest appraised;**

Comment: The statement of the real property rights being appraised must be substantiated, as needed, by copies or summaries of title descriptions or other documents that set forth any known encumbrances.

(v)   **state the type and definition of value and cite the source of the definition;**

Comment: Stating the definition of value also requires any comments needed to clearly indicate to the intended users how the definition is being applied.[26]

When reporting an opinion of market value, state whether the opinion of value is:

- in terms of cash or of financing terms equivalent to cash, or
- based on non-market financing or financing with unusual conditions or incentives.

When an opinion of market value is not in terms of cash or based on financing terms equivalent to cash, summarize the terms of such financing and explain their contributions to or negative influence on value.

The date of report is usually the date of transmittal letter. Either way, the appraiser *must* make the distinction between the dates.

(vi)   **state the effective date of the appraisal and the date of the report;[27]**

Comment: The effective date of the appraisal establishes the context for the value opinion, while the date of the report indicates whether the perspective of the appraiser on the market or property use conditions as of the effective date of the appraisal was prospective, current, or retrospective.

(vii)   **summarize the scope of work used to develop the appraisal;[28]**

Comment: Because intended users' reliance on an appraisal may be affected by the scope of work, the report must enable them to be properly informed and not misled. Sufficient information includes disclosure of research and analyses performed and might also include disclosure of research and analyses not performed.

If significant assistance is given by another individual, the appraiser *must* disclose such assistance.

When any portion of the work involves significant real property appraisal assistance, the appraiser must summarize the extent of that assistance. The signing appraiser must also state the name(s) of those providing the significant real property appraisal assistance in the certification, in accordance with SR 2-3.

(viii)   **summarize the information analyzed, the appraisal methods and techniques employed, and the reasoning that supports the analyses, opinions, and conclusions; exclusion of the sales comparison approach, cost approach, or income approach must be explained;**

Comment: A Summary Appraisal Report must include sufficient information to indicate that the appraiser complied with the requirements of STANDARD 1. The amount of detail required will vary with the significance of the information to the appraisal.

The appraiser must provide sufficient information to enable the client and intended users to understand the rationale for the opinions and conclusions, including reconciliation of the data and approaches, in accordance with Standards Rule 1-6.

When reporting an opinion of market value, a summary of the results of analyzing the subject sales, options, and listings in accordance with Standards Rule 1-5 is required. If such information is unobtainable, a statement on the efforts undertaken by the appraiser to obtain the information is required. If such information is irrelevant, a statement acknowledging the existence of the information and citing its lack of relevance is required.

(ix)   **state the use of the real estate existing as of the date of value and the use of the real estate reflected in the appraisal; and, when an opinion of highest and best use was developed by the appraiser, summarize the support and rationale for that opinion;**

(x)   **clearly and conspicuously:**

- **state all extraordinary assumptions and hypothetical conditions; and**
- **state that their use might have affected the assignment results; and**

(xi)   **include a signed certification in accordance with Standards Rule 2-3.**

Like the self-contained and summary reporting options, the restricted use option has performance requirements. The main difference to note is that a restricted use report is restricted to the client only.

(c)   **The content of a Restricted Use Appraisal Report must be consistent with the intended use of the appraisal and, at a minimum:**

(i)   **state the identity of the client, by name or type;[29] and state a prominent use restriction that limits use of the report to the client and warns that the appraiser's opinions and conclusions set forth in the report may not be understood properly without additional information in the appraiser's workfile;**

Comment: An appraiser must use care when identifying the client to ensure a clear understanding and to avoid violations of the Confidentiality section of the ETHICS RULE. In those rare instances when the client wishes to remain anonymous, an appraiser must still document the identity of the client in the workfile but may omit the client's identity in the report.

While a restricted use report is for the client's use only, an appraiser has an obligation to establish with the client the restrictions placed on the use of the report and the circumstances under such restrictions.

The Restricted Use Appraisal Report is for client use only. Before entering into an agreement, the appraiser should establish with the client the situations where this type of report is to be used and should ensure that the client understands the restricted utility of the Restricted Use Appraisal Report.

(ii)   **state the intended use of the appraisal;**[30]

Comment: The intended use of the appraisal must be consistent with the limitation on use of the Restricted Use Appraisal Report option in this Standards Rule (i.e., client use only).

(iii)   **state information sufficient to identify the real estate involved in the appraisal;**[31]

Comment: The real estate involved in the appraisal can be specified, for example, by a legal description, address, map reference, copy of a survey or map, property sketch, and/or photographs or the like.

(iv)   **state the real property interest appraised;**

(v)   **state the type of value, and cite the source of its definition;**[32]

(vi)   **state the effective date of the appraisal and the date of the report;**[33]

Comment: The effective date of the appraisal establishes the context for the value opinion, while the date of the report indicates whether the perspective of the appraiser on the market or property use conditions as of the effective date of the appraisal was prospective, current, or retrospective.

(vii)   **state the scope of work used to develop the appraisal;**[34]

Comment: Because the client's reliance on an appraisal may be affected by the scope of work, the report must enable them to be properly informed and not misled. Sufficient information includes disclosure of research and analyses performed and might also include disclosure of research and analyses not performed.

If significant assistance is given by another individual, the appraiser *must* disclose such assistance.

When any portion of the work involves significant real property appraisal assistance, the appraiser must state the extent of that assistance. The signing appraiser must also state the name(s) of those providing the significant real property appraisal assistance in the certification, in accordance with SR 2-3.

(viii)   **state the appraisal methods and techniques employed, state the value opinion(s) and conclusion(s) reached, and reference the workfile; exclusion of the sales comparison approach, cost approach, or income approach must be explained;**

Comment: An appraiser must maintain a specific, coherent workfile in support of a Restricted Use Appraisal Report. The contents of the workfile must include sufficient information to indicate that the appraiser complied with the requirements of STANDARD 1 and for the appraiser to produce a Summary Appraisal Report. The file must be available for inspection by the client (or the client's representatives, such as those engaged to complete an appraisal review), state enforcement agencies, such third parties as may be authorized by due process of law, and a duly authorized professional peer review committee except when such disclosure to a committee would violate applicable law or regulation.

When reporting an opinion of market value, information analyzed in compliance with Standards Rule 1-5 is significant information that must be disclosed in a Restricted Use Appraisal Report. If such information is unobtainable, a statement on the efforts undertaken by the appraiser to obtain the information is required. If such information is irrelevant, a statement acknowledging the existence of the information and citing its lack of relevance is required.

(ix)   **state the use of the real estate existing as of the date of value and the use of the real estate reflected in the appraisal; and, when an opinion of highest and best use was developed by the appraiser, state that opinion;**

(x)   **clearly and conspicuously:**

- **state all extraordinary assumptions and hypothetical conditions; and**
- **state that their use might have affected the assignment results; and**

(xi)   **include a signed certification in accordance with Standards Rule 2-3.**

Each written report must have a signed certification.

Standards Rule 2-3

Each written real property appraisal report must contain a signed certification that is similar in content to the following form:

I certify that, to the best of my knowledge and belief:

— **the statements of fact contained in this report are true and correct.**

— **the reported analyses, opinions, and conclusions are limited only by the reported assumptions and limiting conditions and are my personal, impartial, and unbiased professional analyses, opinions, and conclusions.**

— **I have no (or the specified) present or prospective interest in the property that is the subject of this report and no (or the specified) personal interest with respect to the parties involved.**

— **I have no bias with respect to the property that is the subject of this report or to the parties involved with this assignment.**

— **my engagement in this assignment was not contingent upon developing or reporting predetermined results.**

— my compensation for completing this assignment is not contingent upon the development or reporting of a predetermined value or direction in value that favors the cause of the client, the amount of the value opinion, the attainment of a stipulated result, or the occurrence of a subsequent event directly related to the intended use of this appraisal.

— my analyses, opinions, and conclusions were developed, and this report has been prepared, in conformity with the *Uniform Standards of Professional Appraisal Practice.*

— I have (or have not) made a personal inspection of the property that is the subject of this report. (If more than one person signs this certification, the certification must clearly specify which individuals did and which individuals did not make a personal inspection of the appraised property.)[35]

— no one provided significant real property appraisal assistance to the person signing this certification. (If there are exceptions, the name of each individual providing significant real property appraisal assistance must be stated.)

Comment: A signed certification is an integral part of the appraisal report. An appraiser who signs any part of the appraisal report, including a letter of transmittal, must also sign this certification.

In an assignment that includes only assignment results developed by the real property appraiser(s), any appraiser(s) who signs a certification accepts full responsibility for all elements of the certification, for the assignment results, and for the contents of the appraisal report. In an assignment that includes personal property, business or intangible asset assignment results not developed by the real property appraiser(s), any real property appraiser(s) who signs a certification accepts full responsibility for the real property elements of the certification, for the real property assignment results, and for the real property contents of the appraisal report.

When a signing appraiser(s) has relied on work done by others who do not sign the certification, the signing appraiser is responsible for the decision to rely on their work. The signing appraiser(s) is required to have a reasonable basis for believing that those individuals performing the work are competent. The signing appraiser(s) also must have no reason to doubt that the work of those individuals is credible.[36]

The names of individuals providing significant real property appraisal assistance who do not sign a certification must be stated in the certification. It is not required that the description of their assistance be contained in the certification, but disclosure of their assistance is required in accordance with SR 2-2(a), (b), or (c)(vii), as applicable.

Standards Rule 2-4

To the extent that it is both possible and appropriate, an oral real property appraisal report must address the substantive matters set forth in Standards Rule 2-2(b).

Comment: See the Record Keeping section of the ETHICS RULE for corresponding requirements.

■ In Practice

A client recently requested an appraisal involving a property type with which the appraiser has *not* had prior experience or knowledge. The appraiser immediately notified the client of his lack of experience and explained to the client the steps he would take to complete the assignment in a competent manner. The appraiser took all of the steps necessary, but neglected to mention them in his report. Has there been a violation of *USPAP?*

Solution:

Yes. The competency provision requires that the appraiser disclose the steps taken in the report. This would be a violation of the Competency Rule. Remember that to disclose typically means to include the information in the reporting portion of the appraisal process.

■ In Practice

A client recently requested an appraisal involving an older Victorian-style single-family residence. The appraiser determined that because the property is older a cost approach is *not* applicable and not necessary, and did not complete a cost approach. Has there been a violation?

Solution:

No. The appraiser must determine if the approach is applicable or necessary to return credible assignment results. If it is determined that the approach is *not* applicable, as in this case, then the appraiser is not required to perform the approach. However, the appraiser must disclose in the report that the approach is not necessary and therefore has not been performed.

The appraiser *does* have the burden of proof to support the decision that the approach is *not* applicable or, if it is applicable, that to not perform the approach would still yield credible assignment results.

LESSON 3 REVIEW QUESTIONS

1. When reporting the results of a real property appraisal, an appraiser must communicate each analysis, opinion, and conclusion in a manner that is not _____.

2. The essential difference among the three reporting options is in the _____ and level of information provided.

3. Each written real property appraisal report must contain a(n) _____ certification.

4. An appraiser must certify as to whether he or she has _____ the property.

5. Remember that the scope of work decision must match the client's needs and _____ of the report.

6. Identify the client and any intended users, by name or _____.

7. The appraiser must clearly and _____ state all extraordinary assumptions and hypothetical conditions.

8. An appraiser must describe the scope of work used to _____ the appraisal.

9. The restricted use appraisal report is for _____ use only.

10. The three report options are self-contained, summary, and restricted use, where an appraiser must describe, summarize, and _____.

LESSON 3 REVIEW ANSWERS

1. misleading

2. content

3. signed

4. inspected

5. intended use

6. type

7. conspicuously

8. develop

9. client

10. state

SECTION 2 REVIEW QUESTIONS

1. Communication is
   a. the sharing of knowledge between sender and receiver through messages.
   b. a skill that must be honed and constantly developed to be truly effective.
   c. Both a and b
   d. Neither a nor b

2. Effective communication is the sharing of knowledge with a(n) _____ in mind.
   a. client
   b. audience
   c. fifth grader
   d. None of the above

3. For communication to take place
   a. the sender must begin with a notion or a thought, which is translated to a message within the sender's mind.
   b. the message is transferred to a medium such as a written document, an oral statement, or some other form.
   c. the message is delivered to the receiver.
   d. All of the above

4. Which step(s) is/are involved in the effective communication process?
   a. Assess the audience
   b. Appeal to the audience
   c. Revise, edit, and proofread message
   d. All of the above

5. Words or terms that should be avoided in a report include
   a. acronyms.
   b. specialized definitions.
   c. Both a and b
   d. Neither a nor b

6. Visual illustrations include
   a. metaphors.
   b. anecdotes.
   c. photos.
   d. analogies.

7. Verbal illustrations include
   a. maps.
   b. photos.
   c. famous quotes.
   d. charts.

8. The possible expertise levels of an audience include the
   a. uninformed audience and the acquainted audience.
   b. informed audience.
   c. expert audience.
   d. All of the above

9. Industry jargon should
   a. always be avoided.
   b. always be used.
   c. be used whenever possible.
   d. None of the above

10. Which is *NOT* true about writing techniques?
    a. The use of acronyms is acceptable if you define the acronym the first time you use it before repeating it throughout your writing.
    b. Writing should be complicated. Long is better than short, complex is always better than simple.
    c. All procedures or processes should be described in an easy, step-by-step manner.
    d. All main points should be highlighted.

11. The three report options are
    a. self-contained, summary, and restricted use.
    b. complete, limited, and self-sufficient.
    c. descriptive, subjective, and objective.
    d. None of the above

12. The restricted use appraisal report is for _____ use only.
    a. homeowner
    b. client
    c. appraiser
    d. All of the above

13. Each written real property appraisal report must contain a(n) _____ certification.
    a. printed
    b. signed
    c. verbal
    d. faxed

section three

FORM REPORTING

LEARNING OBJECTIVES

By the end of this section, participants will be able to

- be familiar with the Uniform Residential Appraisal Report (URAR);

- be familiar with the history of the URAR;

- be familiar with the required exhibits; and

- describe the use of the URAR.

KEY TERMS

Uniform Residential Appraisal Report (URAR)

LESSON 1: Form 1004—The Uniform Residential Appraisal Report (URAR)

In the 1970s, Fannie Mae and Freddie Mac created a residential appraisal report form to be used by appraisers. The residential report form was entitled the **Uniform Residential Appraisal Report (URAR)**. The URAR was revised in 1975, 1979, and 1986. In 1987, several government agencies, including the Department of Housing and Urban Development (HUD), the Department of Veterans Affairs (VA), and the Farmers Home Administration (now known as Rural Housing Service [RHS]), required the use of the URAR. In 1993, the form was revised again to recognize the *Uniform Standards of Professional Appraisal Practice (USPAP)* as the minimum standard in the real estate appraisal profession. The most recent version of the form became available in March 2005 and became the required form for all Fannie Mae appraisals in November 2005.

The URAR summarizes the appraiser's findings as they perform the necessary and applicable steps in the appraisal process. The URAR is used for a single-family (one-unit) property, a one-unit property with an accessory unit, or a one-unit property located in a planned unit development (PUD). The URAR is not used to report the appraisal of a manufactured home, a condominium unit, or a cooperative project.

Currently, the URAR has six pages in addition to required exhibits. The sections included on each of the first six pages are detailed below.

Page 1 (See Figure 3.1.)

- Subject
- Contract
- Neighborhood
- Site
- Improvements

Page 2 (See Figure 3.2.)

- Sales comparison approach
- Reconciliation

Page 3 (See Figure 3.3.)

- Additional comments
- Cost approach
- Income
- PUD information

Page 4 (See Figure 3.4.)

- Scope of work
- Intended use
- Intended user
- Definition of market value
- Statement of assumptions and limiting conditions

Page 5 (See Figure 3.5.)

- Appraiser's certification

Page 6 (See Figure 3.6.)

- Appraiser's certification (cont'd.)
- Supervisory appraiser's certification
- Appraiser information
- Supervisory appraiser information

Required Exhibits (See Figure 3.7.)

In addition to the first six pages, there are required exhibits, which include:

- A sketch indicating dimensions of the exterior building as well as the calculations used to determine gross living area (GLA). If the subject has an atypical floor plan or a functionally obsolete floor plan (functional obsolescence due to the market's negative response to an atypical floor plan), then a sketch of the interior floor plan is to be included.
- Clear black and white or color photos that show the front elevation, the rear elevation, and the street view of the subject. Photos must be originals that are produced by either photography or electronic imaging.

- Clear black and white or color photos that show the front elevation of each comparable sale. Photos must be originals that are produced by either photography or electronic imaging.

- Any attachments or addendums necessary to support the opinion of market value.

OTHER REPORT FORMS

This section covers only the URAR; however, other report forms also mandated by Fannie Mae are used depending on the type of residential property that is appraised (see the Appendix). Some commonly used report forms and their uses follow:

- **Form 1025—Small Residential Income Property Appraisal.** This report form is used to report an appraisal of two- to four-unit properties, including a two- to four-unit property located within a planned unit development (PUD).

- **Form 216—Operating Income Statement.** A required exhibit when Form 1025 is used. Used in evaluating the applicant's credit on applications for conventional mortgages secured by one-family investment properties and used for all two- to four-family properties, regardless of whether it's owner-occupied.

- **Form 1073—Individual Condominium Unit Appraisal Report.** This report form is used to report an appraisal of a unit in a condominium project located within a planned unit development (PUD).

- **Form 1007—Single-Family Comparable Rent Schedule.** Used to report market rent for a conventional single-family investment property.

FIGURE 3.1
Page 1 of the URAR

Uniform Residential Appraisal Report   File

The purpose of this summary appraisal report is to provide the lender/client with an accurate, and adequately supported, opinion of the market value of the subject property.

SUBJECT

Property Address		City		State	Zip Code
Borrower	Owner of Public Record			County	

Legal Description

Assessor's Parcel #	Tax Year	R.E. Taxes $
Neighborhood Name	Map Reference	Census Tract

Occupant ☐ Owner ☐ Tenant ☐ Vacant   Special Assessments $ ☐ PUD   HOA $ ☐ per year ☐ per month

Property Rights Appraised ☐ Fee Simple ☐ Leasehold ☐ Other (describe)

Assignment Type ☐ Purchase Transaction ☐ Refinance Transaction ☐ Other (describe)

Lender/Client   Address

Is the subject property currently offered for sale or has it been offered for sale in the twelve months prior to the effective date of this appraisal? ☐ Yes ☐ No

Report data source(s) used, offering price(s), and date(s).

CONTRACT

I ☐ did ☐ did not analyze the contract for sale for the subject purchase transaction. Explain the results of the analysis of the contract for sale or why the analysis was not performed.

Contract Price $ Date of Contract   Is the property seller the owner of public record? ☐ Yes ☐ No Data Source(s)

Is there any financial assistance (loan charges, sale concessions, gift or downpayment assistance, etc.) to be paid by any party on behalf of the borrower? ☐ Yes ☐ No
If Yes, report the total dollar amount and describe the items to be paid.

NEIGHBORHOOD

Note: Race and the racial composition of the neighborhood are not appraisal factors.

Neighborhood Characteristics			One-Unit Housing Trends			One-Unit Housing		Present Land Use %	
Location ☐ Urban	☐ Suburban	☐ Rural	Property Values ☐ Increasing	☐ Stable	☐ Declining	PRICE	AGE	One-Unit	%
Built-Up ☐ Over 75%	☐ 25–75%	☐ Under 25%	Demand/Supply ☐ Shortage	☐ In Balance	☐ Over Supply	$ (000)	(yrs)	2-4 Unit	%
Growth ☐ Rapid	☐ Stable	☐ Slow	Marketing Time ☐ Under 3 mths	☐ 3–6 mths	☐ Over 6 mths	Low		Multi-Family	%
Neighborhood Boundaries						High		Commercial	%
						Pred.		Other	%

Neighborhood Description

Market Conditions (including support for the above conclusions)

SITE

Dimensions		Area	Shape	View
Specific Zoning Classification		Zoning Description		

Zoning Compliance ☐ Legal ☐ Legal Nonconforming (Grandfathered Use) ☐ No Zoning ☐ Illegal (describe)

Is the highest and best use of the subject property as improved (or as proposed per plans and specifications) the present use? ☐ Yes ☐ No If No, describe

Utilities	Public	Other (describe)		Public	Other (describe)	Off-site Improvements—Type	Public	Private
Electricity	☐	☐	Water	☐	☐	Street	☐	☐
Gas	☐	☐	Sanitary Sewer	☐	☐	Alley	☐	☐

FEMA Special Flood Hazard Area ☐ Yes ☐ No FEMA Flood Zone   FEMA Map #   FEMA Map Date

Are the utilities and off-site improvements typical for the market area? ☐ Yes ☐ No If No, describe

Are there any adverse site conditions or external factors (easements, encroachments, environmental conditions, land uses, etc.)? ☐ Yes ☐ No If Yes, describe

IMPROVEMENTS

General Description		Foundation		Exterior Description	materials/condition	Interior	materials/condition
Units ☐ One ☐ One with Accessory Unit		☐ Concrete Slab ☐ Crawl Space		Foundation Walls		Floors	
# of Stories		☐ Full Basement ☐ Partial Basement		Exterior Walls		Walls	
Type ☐ Det. ☐ Att. ☐ S-Det./End Unit		Basement Area sq. ft.		Roof Surface		Trim/Finish	
☐ Existing ☐ Proposed ☐ Under Const.		Basement Finish %		Gutters & Downspouts		Bath Floor	
Design (Style)		☐ Outside Entry/Exit ☐ Sump Pump		Window Type		Bath Wainscot	
Year Built		Evidence of ☐ Infestation		Storm Sash/Insulated		Car Storage ☐ None	
Effective Age (Yrs)		☐ Dampness ☐ Settlement		Screens		☐ Driveway # of Cars	
Attic ☐ None		Heating ☐ FWA ☐ HWBB ☐ Radiant		Amenities ☐ Woodstove(s) #		Driveway Surface	
☐ Drop Stair ☐ Stairs		☐ Other Fuel		☐ Fireplace(s) # ☐ Fence		☐ Garage # of Cars	
☐ Floor ☐ Scuttle		Cooling ☐ Central Air Conditioning		☐ Patio/Deck ☐ Porch		☐ Carport # of Cars	
☐ Finished ☐ Heated		☐ Individual ☐ Other		☐ Pool ☐ Other		☐ Att. ☐ Det. ☐ Built-in	

Appliances ☐ Refrigerator ☐ Range/Oven ☐ Dishwasher ☐ Disposal ☐ Microwave ☐ Washer/Dryer ☐ Other (describe)

Finished area **above** grade contains: Rooms   Bedrooms   Bath(s)   Square Feet of Gross Living Area Above Grade

Additional features (special energy efficient items, etc.)

Describe the condition of the property (including needed repairs, deterioration, renovations, remodeling, etc.).

Are there any physical deficiencies or adverse conditions that affect the livability, soundness, or structural integrity of the property? ☐ Yes ☐ No If Yes, describe

Does the property generally conform to the neighborhood (functional utility, style, condition, use, construction, etc.)? ☐ Yes ☐ No If No, describe

FIGURE 3.2
Page 2 of the URAR

Uniform Residential Appraisal Report

File #

| There are | comparable properties currently offered for sale in the subject neighborhood ranging in price from $ | | | to $ | |
| There are | comparable sales in the subject neighborhood within the past twelve months ranging in sale price from $ | | | to $ | |

FEATURE	SUBJECT	COMPARABLE SALE # 1		COMPARABLE SALE # 2		COMPARABLE SALE # 3	
Address							
Proximity to Subject							
Sale Price	$		$		$		$
Sale Price/Gross Liv. Area	$ sq. ft.	$ sq. ft.		$ sq. ft.		$ sq. ft.	
Data Source(s)							
Verification Source(s)							
VALUE ADJUSTMENTS	DESCRIPTION	DESCRIPTION	+(-) $ Adjustment	DESCRIPTION	+(-) $ Adjustment	DESCRIPTION	+(-) $ Adjustment
Sale or Financing Concessions							
Date of Sale/Time							
Location							
Leasehold/Fee Simple							
Site							
View							
Design (Style)							
Quality of Construction							
Actual Age							
Condition							
Above Grade	Total Bdrms. Baths	Total Bdrms. Baths		Total Bdrms. Baths		Total Bdrms. Baths	
Room Count							
Gross Living Area	sq. ft.	sq. ft.		sq. ft.		sq. ft.	
Basement & Finished Rooms Below Grade							
Functional Utility							
Heating/Cooling							
Energy Efficient Items							
Garage/Carport							
Porch/Patio/Deck							
Net Adjustment (Total)		☐ + ☐ -	$	☐ + ☐ -	$	☐ + ☐ -	$
Adjusted Sale Price of Comparables		Net Adj. % Gross Adj. %	$	Net Adj. % Gross Adj. %	$	Net Adj. % Gross Adj. %	$

I ☐ did ☐ did not research the sale or transfer history of the subject property and comparable sales. If not, explain

My research ☐ did ☐ did not reveal any prior sales or transfers of the subject property for the three years prior to the effective date of this appraisal.

Data source(s)

My research ☐ did ☐ did not reveal any prior sales or transfers of the comparable sales for the year prior to the date of sale of the comparable sale.

Data source(s)

Report the results of the research and analysis of the prior sale or transfer history of the subject property and comparable sales (report additional prior sales on page 3).

ITEM	SUBJECT	COMPARABLE SALE # 1	COMPARABLE SALE # 2	COMPARABLE SALE # 3
Date of Prior Sale/Transfer				
Price of Prior Sale/Transfer				
Data Source(s)				
Effective Date of Data Source(s)				

Analysis of prior sale or transfer history of the subject property and comparable sales

Summary of Sales Comparison Approach

Indicated Value by Sales Comparison Approach $

Indicated Value by: Sales Comparison Approach $ Cost Approach (if developed) $ Income Approach (if developed) $

This appraisal is made ☐ "as is", ☐ subject to completion per plans and specifications on the basis of a hypothetical condition that the improvements have been completed, ☐ subject to the following repairs or alterations on the basis of a hypothetical condition that the repairs or alterations have been completed, or ☐ subject to the following required inspection based on the extraordinary assumption that the condition or deficiency does not require alteration or repair:

Based on a complete visual inspection of the interior and exterior areas of the subject property, defined scope of work, statement of assumptions and limiting conditions, and appraiser's certification, my (our) opinion of the market value, as defined, of the real property that is the subject of this report is $, as of   , which is the date of inspection and the effective date of this appraisal.

(Left margin vertical labels: SALES COMPARISON APPROACH, RECONCILIATION)

FIGURE 3.3
Page 3 of the URAR

Uniform Residential Appraisal Report

File #

ADDITIONAL COMMENTS

COST APPROACH TO VALUE (not required by Fannie Mae)

Provide adequate information for the lender/client to replicate the below cost figures and calculations.

Support for the opinion of site value (summary of comparable land sales or other methods for estimating site value)

COST APPROACH	
ESTIMATED ☐ REPRODUCTION OR ☐ REPLACEMENT COST NEW	OPINION OF SITE VALUE .... = $
Source of cost data	Dwelling Sq. Ft. @ $ .... =$
Quality rating from cost service Effective date of cost data	Sq. Ft. @ $ .... =$
Comments on Cost Approach (gross living area calculations, depreciation, etc.)	
	Garage/Carport Sq. Ft. @ $ .... =$
	Total Estimate of Cost-New .... = $
	Less Physical Functional External
	Depreciation =$( )
	Depreciated Cost of Improvements............................ =$
	"As-is" Value of Site Improvements........................... =$
Estimated Remaining Economic Life (HUD and VA only) Years	Indicated Value By Cost Approach .... =$

INCOME APPROACH TO VALUE (not required by Fannie Mae)

INCOME	
Estimated Monthly Market Rent $ X Gross Rent Multiplier = $ Indicated Value by Income Approach	
Summary of Income Approach (including support for market rent and GRM)	

PROJECT INFORMATION FOR PUDs (if applicable)

PUD INFORMATION

Is the developer/builder in control of the Homeowners' Association (HOA)? ☐ Yes ☐ No   Unit type(s) ☐ Detached ☐ Attached

Provide the following information for PUDs ONLY if the developer/builder is in control of the HOA and the subject property is an attached dwelling unit.

Legal name of project

Total number of phases   Total number of units   Total number of units sold

Total number of units rented   Total number of units for sale   Data source(s)

Was the project created by the conversion of an existing building(s) into a PUD? ☐ Yes ☐ No   If Yes, date of conversion

Does the project contain any multi-dwelling units? ☐ Yes ☐ No   Data source(s)

Are the units, common elements, and recreation facilities complete? ☐ Yes ☐ No   If No, describe the status of completion.

Are the common elements leased to or by the Homeowners' Association? ☐ Yes ☐ No   If Yes, describe the rental terms and options.

Describe common elements and recreational facilities

FIGURE 3.4
Page 4 of the URAR

Uniform Residential Appraisal Report   File

This report form is designed to report an appraisal of a one-unit property or a one-unit property with an accessory unit; including a unit in a planned unit development (PUD). This report form is not designed to report an appraisal of a manufactured home or a unit in a condominium or cooperative project.

This appraisal report is subject to the following scope of work, intended use, intended user, definition of market value, statement of assumptions and limiting conditions, and certifications. Modifications, additions, or deletions to the intended use, intended user, definition of market value, or assumptions and limiting conditions are not permitted. The appraiser may expand the scope of work to include any additional research or analysis necessary based on the complexity of this appraisal assignment. Modifications or deletions to the certifications are also not permitted. However, additional certifications that do not constitute material alterations to this appraisal report, such as those required by law or those related to the appraiser's continuing education or membership in an appraisal organization, are permitted.

SCOPE OF WORK: The scope of work for this appraisal is defined by the complexity of this appraisal assignment and the reporting requirements of this appraisal report form, including the following definition of market value, statement of assumptions and limiting conditions, and certifications. The appraiser must, at a minimum: (1) perform a complete visual inspection of the interior and exterior areas of the subject property, (2) inspect the neighborhood, (3) inspect each of the comparable sales from at least the street, (4) research, verify, and analyze data from reliable public and/or private sources, and (5) report his or her analysis, opinions, and conclusions in this appraisal report.

INTENDED USE: The intended use of this appraisal report is for the lender/client to evaluate the property that is the subject of this appraisal for a mortgage finance transaction.

INTENDED USER: The intended user of this appraisal report is the lender/client.

DEFINITION OF MARKET VALUE: The most probable price which a property should bring in a competitive and open market under all conditions requisite to a fair sale, the buyer and seller, each acting prudently, knowledgeably and assuming the price is not affected by undue stimulus. Implicit in this definition is the consummation of a sale as of a specified date and the passing of title from seller to buyer under conditions whereby: (1) buyer and seller are typically motivated; (2) both parties are well informed or well advised, and each acting in what he or she considers his or her own best interest; (3) a reasonable time is allowed for exposure in the open market; (4) payment is made in terms of cash in U. S. dollars or in terms of financial arrangements comparable thereto; and (5) the price represents the normal consideration for the property sold unaffected by special or creative financing or sales concessions* granted by anyone associated with the sale.

*Adjustments to the comparables must be made for special or creative financing or sales concessions. No adjustments are necessary for those costs which are normally paid by sellers as a result of tradition or law in a market area; these costs are readily identifiable since the seller pays these costs in virtually all sales transactions. Special or creative financing adjustments can be made to the comparable property by comparisons to financing terms offered by a third party institutional lender that is not already involved in the property or transaction. Any adjustment should not be calculated on a mechanical dollar for dollar cost of the financing or concession but the dollar amount of any adjustment should approximate the market's reaction to the financing or concessions based on the appraiser's judgment.

STATEMENT OF ASSUMPTIONS AND LIMITING CONDITIONS: The appraiser's certification in this report is subject to the following assumptions and limiting conditions:

1. The appraiser will not be responsible for matters of a legal nature that affect either the property being appraised or the title to it, except for information that he or she became aware of during the research involved in performing this appraisal. The appraiser assumes that the title is good and marketable and will not render any opinions about the title.

2. The appraiser has provided a sketch in this appraisal report to show the approximate dimensions of the improvements. The sketch is included only to assist the reader in visualizing the property and understanding the appraiser's determination of its size.

3. The appraiser has examined the available flood maps that are provided by the Federal Emergency Management Agency (or other data sources) and has noted in this appraisal report whether any portion of the subject site is located in an identified Special Flood Hazard Area. Because the appraiser is not a surveyor, he or she makes no guarantees, express or implied, regarding this determination.

4. The appraiser will not give testimony or appear in court because he or she made an appraisal of the property in question, unless specific arrangements to do so have been made beforehand, or as otherwise required by law.

5. The appraiser has noted in this appraisal report any adverse conditions (such as needed repairs, deterioration, the presence of hazardous wastes, toxic substances, etc.) observed during the inspection of the subject property or that he or she became aware of during the research involved in performing this appraisal. Unless otherwise stated in this appraisal report, the appraiser has no knowledge of any hidden or unapparent physical deficiencies or adverse conditions of the property (such as, but not limited to, needed repairs, deterioration, the presence of hazardous wastes, toxic substances, adverse environmental conditions, etc.) that would make the property less valuable, and has assumed that there are no such conditions and makes no guarantees or warranties, express or implied. The appraiser will not be responsible for any such conditions that do exist or for any engineering or testing that might be required to discover whether such conditions exist. Because the appraiser is not an expert in the field of environmental hazards, this appraisal report must not be considered as an environmental assessment of the property.

6. The appraiser has based his or her appraisal report and valuation conclusion for an appraisal that is subject to satisfactory completion, repairs, or alterations on the assumption that the completion, repairs, or alterations of the subject property will be performed in a professional manner.

FIGURE 3.5
Page 5 of the URAR

Uniform Residential Appraisal Report   File

APPRAISER'S CERTIFICATION: The Appraiser certifies and agrees that:

1. I have, at a minimum, developed and reported this appraisal in accordance with the scope of work requirements stated in this appraisal report.

2. I performed a complete visual inspection of the interior and exterior areas of the subject property. I reported the condition of the improvements in factual, specific terms. I identified and reported the physical deficiencies that could affect the livability, soundness, or structural integrity of the property.

3. I performed this appraisal in accordance with the requirements of the Uniform Standards of Professional Appraisal Practice that were adopted and promulgated by the Appraisal Standards Board of The Appraisal Foundation and that were in place at the time this appraisal report was prepared.

4. I developed my opinion of the market value of the real property that is the subject of this report based on the sales comparison approach to value. I have adequate comparison market data to develop a reliable sales comparison approach for this appraisal assignment. I further certify that I considered the cost and income approaches to value but did not develop them, unless otherwise indicated in this report.

5. I researched, verified, analyzed, and reported on any current agreement for sale for the subject property, any offering for sale of the subject property in the twelve months prior to the effective date of this appraisal, and the prior sales of the subject property for a minimum of three years prior to the effective date of this appraisal, unless otherwise indicated in this report.

6. I researched, verified, analyzed, and reported on the prior sales of the comparable sales for a minimum of one year prior to the date of sale of the comparable sale, unless otherwise indicated in this report.

7. I selected and used comparable sales that are locationally, physically, and functionally the most similar to the subject property.

8. I have not used comparable sales that were the result of combining a land sale with the contract purchase price of a home that has been built or will be built on the land.

9. I have reported adjustments to the comparable sales that reflect the market's reaction to the differences between the subject property and the comparable sales.

10. I verified, from a disinterested source, all information in this report that was provided by parties who have a financial interest in the sale or financing of the subject property.

11. I have knowledge and experience in appraising this type of property in this market area.

12. I am aware of, and have access to, the necessary and appropriate public and private data sources, such as multiple listing services, tax assessment records, public land records and other such data sources for the area in which the property is located.

13. I obtained the information, estimates, and opinions furnished by other parties and expressed in this appraisal report from reliable sources that I believe to be true and correct.

14. I have taken into consideration the factors that have an impact on value with respect to the subject neighborhood, subject property, and the proximity of the subject property to adverse influences in the development of my opinion of market value. I have noted in this appraisal report any adverse conditions (such as, but not limited to, needed repairs, deterioration, the presence of hazardous wastes, toxic substances, adverse environmental conditions, etc.) observed during the inspection of the subject property or that I became aware of during the research involved in performing this appraisal. I have considered these adverse conditions in my analysis of the property value, and have reported on the effect of the conditions on the value and marketability of the subject property.

15. I have not knowingly withheld any significant information from this appraisal report and, to the best of my knowledge, all statements and information in this appraisal report are true and correct.

16. I stated in this appraisal report my own personal, unbiased, and professional analysis, opinions, and conclusions, which are subject only to the assumptions and limiting conditions in this appraisal report.

17. I have no present or prospective interest in the property that is the subject of this report, and I have no present or prospective personal interest or bias with respect to the participants in the transaction. I did not base, either partially or completely, my analysis and/or opinion of market value in this appraisal report on the race, color, religion, sex, age, marital status, handicap, familial status, or national origin of either the prospective owners or occupants of the subject property or of the present owners or occupants of the properties in the vicinity of the subject property or on any other basis prohibited by law.

18. My employment and/or compensation for performing this appraisal or any future or anticipated appraisals was not conditioned on any agreement or understanding, written or otherwise, that I would report (or present analysis supporting) a predetermined specific value, a predetermined minimum value, a range or direction in value, a value that favors the cause of any party, or the attainment of a specific result or occurrence of a specific subsequent event (such as approval of a pending mortgage loan application).

19. I personally prepared all conclusions and opinions about the real estate that were set forth in this appraisal report. If I relied on significant real property appraisal assistance from any individual or individuals in the performance of this appraisal or the preparation of this appraisal report, I have named such individual(s) and disclosed the specific tasks performed in this appraisal report. I certify that any individual so named is qualified to perform the tasks. I have not authorized anyone to make a change to any item in this appraisal report; therefore, any change made to this appraisal is unauthorized and I will take no responsibility for it.

20. I identified the lender/client in this appraisal report who is the individual, organization, or agent for the organization that ordered and will receive this appraisal report.

FIGURE 3.6
Page 6 of the URAR

Uniform Residential Appraisal Report   File

21. The lender/client may disclose or distribute this appraisal report to: the borrower; another lender at the request of the borrower; the mortgagee or its successors and assigns; mortgage insurers; government sponsored enterprises; other secondary market participants; data collection or reporting services; professional appraisal organizations; any department, agency, or instrumentality of the United States; and any state, the District of Columbia, or other jurisdictions; without having to obtain the appraiser's or supervisory appraiser's (if applicable) consent. Such consent must be obtained before this appraisal report may be disclosed or distributed to any other party (including, but not limited to, the public through advertising, public relations, news, sales, or other media).

22. I am aware that any disclosure or distribution of this appraisal report by me or the lender/client may be subject to certain laws and regulations. Further, I am also subject to the provisions of the Uniform Standards of Professional Appraisal Practice that pertain to disclosure or distribution by me.

23. The borrower, another lender at the request of the borrower, the mortgagee or its successors and assigns, mortgage insurers, government sponsored enterprises, and other secondary market participants may rely on this appraisal report as part of any mortgage finance transaction that involves any one or more of these parties.

24. If this appraisal report was transmitted as an "electronic record" containing my "electronic signature," as those terms are defined in applicable federal and/or state laws (excluding audio and video recordings), or a facsimile transmission of this appraisal report containing a copy or representation of my signature, the appraisal report shall be as effective, enforceable and valid as if a paper version of this appraisal report were delivered containing my original hand written signature.

25. Any intentional or negligent misrepresentation(s) contained in this appraisal report may result in civil liability and/or criminal penalties including, but not limited to, fine or imprisonment or both under the provisions of Title 18, United States Code, Section 1001, et seq., or similar state laws.

SUPERVISORY APPRAISER'S CERTIFICATION: The Supervisory Appraiser certifies and agrees that:

1. I directly supervised the appraiser for this appraisal assignment, have read the appraisal report, and agree with the appraiser's analysis, opinions, statements, conclusions, and the appraiser's certification.

2. I accept full responsibility for the contents of this appraisal report including, but not limited to, the appraiser's analysis, opinions, statements, conclusions, and the appraiser's certification.

3. The appraiser identified in this appraisal report is either a sub-contractor or an employee of the supervisory appraiser (or the appraisal firm), is qualified to perform this appraisal, and is acceptable to perform this appraisal under the applicable state law.

4. This appraisal report complies with the Uniform Standards of Professional Appraisal Practice that were adopted and promulgated by the Appraisal Standards Board of The Appraisal Foundation and that were in place at the time this appraisal report was prepared.

5. If this appraisal report was transmitted as an "electronic record" containing my "electronic signature," as those terms are defined in applicable federal and/or state laws (excluding audio and video recordings), or a facsimile transmission of this appraisal report containing a copy or representation of my signature, the appraisal report shall be as effective, enforceable and valid as if a paper version of this appraisal report were delivered containing my original hand written signature.

APPRAISER

Signature _____
Name _____
Company Name _____
Company Address _____

Telephone Number _____
Email Address _____
Date of Signature and Report _____
Effective Date of Appraisal _____
State Certification # _____
or State License # _____
or Other (describe) _____ State # _____
State _____
Expiration Date of Certification or License _____

ADDRESS OF PROPERTY APPRAISED
_____
_____

APPRAISED VALUE OF SUBJECT PROPERTY $ _____
LENDER/CLIENT
Name _____
Company Name _____
Company Address _____
_____
Email Address _____

SUPERVISORY APPRAISER (ONLY IF REQUIRED)

Signature _____
Name _____
Company Name _____
Company Address _____
_____

Telephone Number _____
Email Address _____
Date of Signature _____
State Certification # _____
or State License # _____
State _____
Expiration Date of Certification or License _____

SUBJECT PROPERTY
☐ Did not inspect subject property
☐ Did inspect exterior of subject property from street
    Date of Inspection _____
☐ Did inspect interior and exterior of subject property
    Date of Inspection _____

COMPARABLE SALES
☐ Did not inspect exterior of comparable sales from street
☐ Did inspect exterior of comparable sales from street
    Date of Inspection _____

Freddie Mac Form 70   March 2005   Page 6 of 6   Fannie Mae Form 1004   March 2005

FIGURE 3.7
Required Exhibits

Subject Front

Subject Rear

Subject Street Scene

Comparable #1

Comparable #2

Comparable #3

FIGURE 3.7 (CONTINUED)
Required Exhibits

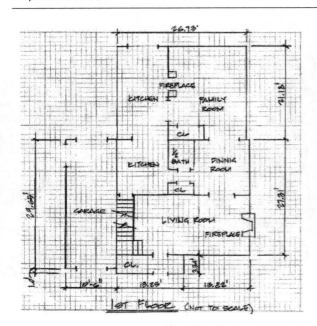

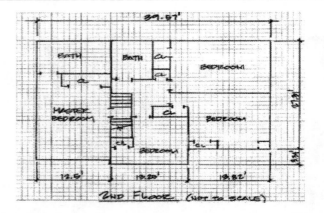

| Gross Building Area (GBA) _____ 3,291 | | |
| Gross Living Area (GLA) _____ 2,299 | | |

Area(s)	Area	% of GBA
Living	2,299	69.86
Level 1	1,247	37.89
Level 2	1,052	31.97
Level 3		
Other		
Basement	681	20.69
Garage	311	9.45

AREA MEASUREMENTS					AREA TYPE					
Measurements		Factor		Total	Level 1	Level 2	Level 3	Other	Bsmt.	Garage
21.18 × 26.73 ×		1	=	566.14	1					
10.50 × 29.65 ×		1	=	311.33						1
27.31 × 26.57 ×		1	=	725.63	1	1			1	
3.34 × −13.32 ×		1	=	−44.49	1	1			1	
12.50 × 29.65 ×		1	=	370.63		1				
× ×			=							
× ×			=							
× ×			=							
× ×			=							
× ×			=							
× ×			=							

FIGURE 3.7 (CONTINUED)
Required Exhibits

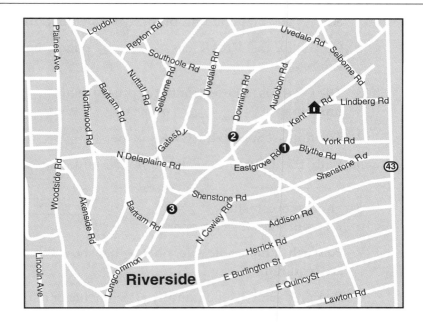

LESSON 1 REVIEW QUESTIONS

1. The URAR is used for a(n) _____ or a one-unit property with a(n) _____ or a one-unit property located in a(n) _____.

2. Currently, the URAR has _____ pages, not including required exhibits.

3. The URAR is not used for the appraisal of a(n) _____ home, _____ unit, or a(n) _____ project.

4. The first section on the URAR is the _____ section.

5. With the URAR, a sketch, photos, and map are considered to be _____.

6. Photos must show _____, _____, and _____ views of the subject property

7. For each comparable sale, photos that show the _____ elevations are required.

8. Required exhibits include any attachments or addendums necessary to support the opinion of _____.

9. The scope of work, intended use, and intended user are located on page ____.

10. The income approach and the cost approach are located on page ____.

LESSON 1 REVIEW ANSWERS

1. single-family; accessory unit; planned unit development

2. six

3. manufactured; condominium; cooperative

4. subject

5. required exhibits

6. front; rear; street

7. front

8. market value

9. 4

10. 3

LESSON 2: The URAR, Page 1

SUBJECT SECTION

Uniform Residential Appraisal Report   File

The purpose of this summary appraisal report is to provide the lender/client with an accurate, and adequately supported, opinion of the market value of the subject property.				
Property Address		City	State	Zip Code
Borrower	Owner of Public Record		County	
Legal Description				
Assessor's Parcel #		Tax Year	R.E. Taxes $	
Neighborhood Name		Map Reference	Census Tract	
Occupant ☐ Owner ☐ Tenant ☐ Vacant	Special Assessments $	☐ PUD HOA $	☐ per year ☐ per month	
Property Rights Appraised ☐ Fee Simple ☐ Leasehold ☐ Other (describe)				
Assignment Type ☐ Purchase Transaction ☐ Refinance Transaction ☐ Other (describe)				
Lender/Client	Address			
Is the subject property currently offered for sale or has it been offered for sale in the twelve months prior to the effective date of this appraisal? ☐ Yes ☐ No				
Report data source(s) used, offering price(s), and date(s).				

File Number   The file number is assigned by either the appraiser or the lender/client.

Property Address   The subject property is identified by the full street address or rural route number. The subject must be identified in such a way that it can be easily located. For example, the use of a post office box number alone is not enough information to sufficiently locate the subject.

City   The name of the city where the subject property is located. For properties that are located outside city limits, the city of the post office serving the subject can be indicated.

State   The full name or the two letter abbreviation of the state in which the subject is located.

Zip Code   The U.S. Postal Service delivery code is entered here.

Borrower   The name of the person(s) acquiring the funds from the lender/client.

Owner of Pubic Record   The current legal owner of the property.

County   The county in which the subject is located.

Legal Description Legal descriptions can be lengthy, and a full legal description of the subject will not likely fit in the space provided. In this case, a separate attachment can be used.

Assessor's Parcel Number The subject property's parcel number assigned by the assessor.

Tax Year The year of the tax information included in the report.

R.E. Taxes ($) The annual real estate taxes due. This information can be obtained from the property owner's most recent real estate tax bill or by contacting the local county tax assessor's or treasurer's office.

Neighborhood Name The name of the neighborhood or subdivision in which the subject is located.

Map Reference The map reference number for the region.

Census Tract The census tract number for the subject. In the United States a census tract is a small statistical subdivision of a county. Census tract data provides population and housing statistics for a specific area. Within one community there may be several census tracts. The census tract number for a particular property address is available online.

Occupant Once the occupant of the subject is verified, the proper box is checked indicating that the subject is owner-occupied, tenant-occupied, or vacant. If vacant, indicate the length of time that the subject property has been vacant in the addendum section of the report.

Special Assessments ($) Any assessments levied against the subject property for roads, sewer, etc.

PUD If the subject property is located within a planned unit development (PUD) this box is checked.

Homeowners' Association ($) If the subject property is located within a PUD and has shared ownership of common areas, the homeowners' association charges either a monthly or annual fee for the upkeep and maintenance of these areas. A clubhouse, swimming pool, green belts, and security posts are all examples of common areas within a PUD.

Property Rights Appraised The property rights that are being appraised are indicated, whether fee simple, leasehold, or other. If the other box is checked, the appraisal results may need to be reported on a different form, such as in the case of individual cooperative units.

Assignment Type   The purpose of the appraisal assignment is indicated, whether a purchase transaction, a refinance transaction, or other. Besides a purchase transaction or refinance transaction, the purpose of the appraisal maybe for the transfer of loan servicing.

Lender/Client   The lender/client name is indicated.

Address   The address of the lender/client is indicated.

Is the subject property currently offered for sale or has it been offered for sale in the 12 months prior to the effective date of this appraisal?   Once this information is verified by the appraiser, the yes or no box is checked.

Report data source(s) used, offering price(s), and date(s).   Data sources and any offering prices or sales of the subject are listed here. Important indicators of the market's acceptance of a particular property are the length of time a property is offered for sale prior to a contract sale and a large difference between the asking price and the contract price.

CONTRACT SECTION

| I ☐ did ☐ did not analyze the contract for sale for the subject purchase transaction. Explain the results of the analysis of the contract for sale or why the analysis was not performed. |
| Contract Price $ Date of Contract   Is the property seller the owner of public record? ☐Yes ☐No   Data Source(s) |
| Is there any financial assistance (loan charges, sale concessions, gift or downpayment assistance, etc.) to be paid by any party on behalf of the borrower? ☐ Yes ☐ No If Yes, report the total dollar amount and describe the items to be paid. |

I did or did not analyze the contract for sale of the subject purchase transaction. Explain the results of the analysis of the contract for sale or why the analysis was not performed.   It is important to understand the mind-set of the purchaser of the subject property; therefore, the final contract price that the purchaser was willing to pay is of great interest to the appraiser.

Contract Price ($)   The sales price indicated on the contract of sale.

Date of Contract   The date that the contract was signed by all parties. If the refinance transaction or other boxes were checked in the subject section, then "N/A Refinance" or "N/A" and the purpose of the appraisal is indicated.

Is the property seller the owner of public record?   After confirming with the county recorder's office, the appraiser indicates if the seller listed on the contract is indeed the same person(s) listed as owner(s) of public record.

Data Source   The source of the contract information is indicated. Examples of data sources include the lender, seller, buyer, or sales broker.

Is there any financial assistance (loan charges, sale concessions, gift or down payment assistance, etc.) to be paid by any party on behalf of the borrower?   The appraiser checks either the yes or no box.

If yes, report the total dollar amount and describe the items to be paid.   After inspecting the sales contract, the appraiser can determine the total dollar amount of any financial assistance. Other documents need to be inspected such as those of any sponsoring organizations that provide gifts to the buyer to be used as down payment after an agreed-upon gift is made to the organization by the seller.

NEIGHBORHOOD SECTION

Note: Race and the racial composition of the neighborhood are not appraisal factors.						
Neighborhood Characteristics			**One-Unit Housing Trends**		**One-Unit Housing**	**Present Land Use %**
Location ☐ Urban ☐ Suburban ☐ Rural			Property Values ☐ Increasing ☐ Stable ☐ Declining		PRICE AGE	One-Unit %
Built-Up ☐ Over 75% ☐ 25–75% ☐ Under 25%			Demand/Supply ☐ Shortage ☐ In Balance ☐ Over Supply		$ (000) (yrs)	2-4 Unit %
Growth ☐ Rapid ☐ Stable ☐ Slow			Marketing Time ☐ Under 3 mths ☐ 3–6 mths ☐ Over 6 mths		Low	Multi-Family %
Neighborhood Boundaries					High	Commercial %
					Pred.	Other %
Neighborhood Description						
Market Conditions (including support for the above conclusions)						

Location   The appraiser determines whether the subject property is located in an urban, suburban, or rural area, and checks the proper box.

Built-Up   The percentage of land within the neighborhood is indicated. If the Under 25% box is checked the appraiser should comment in the comment area or the addendum as to why this is the case.

Growth   The appraiser can confirm growth information with the local building department, which tracks the distribution of building permits. The subject neighborhood is checked against comparable neighborhoods and the proper box is checked.

Property Values   The appraiser can analyze the sales of comparable properties within the subject neighborhood to determine a trend in property values. The proper box is checked here indicating that property values are increasing, stable, or declining. If the declining box is checked then comments should be made in the market condition section explaining this decline in property values. Issues that should be addressed include the number of days a property is on the market, the differences between list price and contract sales price, and so on.

Demand/Supply To determine demand and supply, the appraiser checks the marketing time of properties within the subject neighborhood. If there is a relatively low marketing time, then it can be assumed that there is a potential for greater demand than supply, thus a shortage of one-unit housing. If the rate of listings and sales appears to be equal, then it can be assumed that supply and demand are in balance. If the appraiser notices longer marketing times, then it can be assumed that the demand is less than the supply and, therefore, there is an oversupply of one-unit housing. If the oversupply box is checked, the appraiser needs to comment on the reason for the oversupply and how it will affect the subject's property value.

Marketing Time The appraiser analyzes market data and determines the average length of time it takes to sell one-unit housing in the subject neighborhood. Under-priced housing will sell faster than over-priced housing. Neither situation is an adequate representation of market value. The proper box is checked here indicating a marketing time of either Under 3 months, 3–6 months, or Over 6 months. If the Over 6 months box is check further explanation is needed as it could be an indication of an oversupply of one-unit housing in the neighborhood.

Price The appraiser determines the range of sales prices within the subject neighborhood and eliminates the extreme low and extreme high sales prices in the range of sales prices. The low, high, and predominant sales prices are then indicated.

Age The appraiser determines the range of the ages of one-unit housing within the subject neighborhood and eliminates the extreme low and the extreme high ages. The low, high, and predominant ages in years are then indicated.

Present Land Use The appraiser enters the estimated land use within the subject's neighborhood and enters the percentages in each of the categories. If the appraiser finds that there is a different land use than those listed on the form, for example vacant undeveloped land, then they should indicate the percentage under Other and list this land use in the neighborhood description area.

Neighborhood Boundaries The neighborhood boundaries, such as street boundaries, are listed here. These boundaries should correspond with the map exhibit attached to the report.

Neighborhood Description Both positive and negative features of the subject neighborhood that can potentially affect property value are described here. Features that would be of interest in the minds of potential purchasers and that should be commented on in this section include:

- Employment stability
- Convenience to employment
- Convenience to school
- Convenience to shopping
- Adequacy of public transportation
- Adequacy of utilities
- Police and fire protection
- Protection from detrimental conditions
- Recreation facilities
- Property comparability
- Appeal to market
- General appearance of property

Market Conditions   Positive or negative factors outside the property lines are described here. These factors include the availability of financing and apparent trends in the market.

Interest rates, as well as any special financing arrangements, can affect the sales prices of properties within a specific market. For example, above-market interest rates will result in lower sales prices; conversely, lower-than-market interest rates will result in higher sales prices.

Market trend indicators include the number of properties listed for sale and the length of time before these properties are sold. Reduced demand for properties comparable to the subject will result in an increasing number of properties listed for sale as well as longer marketing times.

Any of these factors that may adversely affect the value of the subject property should be commented on here. The use of an addendum may be necessary as the space here is limited.

SITE SECTION

Dimensions			Area	Shape		View		
Specific Zoning Classification			Zoning Description					
Zoning Compliance ☐ Legal ☐ Legal Nonconforming (Grandfathered Use) ☐ No Zoning ☐ Illegal (describe)								
Is the highest and best use of the subject property as improved (or as proposed per plans and specifications) the present use? ☐ Yes ☐ No If No, describe								
Utilities	Public	Other (describe)		Public	Other (describe)	Off-site Improvements—Type	Public	Private
Electricity	☐	☐	Water	☐	☐	Street	☐	☐
Gas	☐	☐	Sanitary Sewer	☐	☐	Alley	☐	☐
FEMA Special Flood Hazard Area ☐ Yes ☐ No FEMA Flood Zone				FEMA Map #		FEMA Map Date		
Are the utilities and off-site improvements typical for the market area? ☐ Yes ☐ No If No, describe								
Are there any adverse site conditions or external factors (easements, encroachments, environmental conditions, land uses, etc.)? ☐ Yes ☐ No If Yes, describe								

Dimensions   The boundary measurements, in linear feet, of the subject site are indicated (e.g., 50' × 150'). If the site is irregular in shape, then all of the dimensions are reported (e.g., 50' × 135' × 155' × 65').

Area   The land area of the subject site is indicated. The land area is expressed as square footage and if it is greater than one acre (greater than 43,560 square feet), it can be expressed in acres as well. If the size of the subject site is not typical for the area, this also should be indicated here (e.g., "large," "oversized," or "smaller").

Shape   The geometric shape of the site parameter is entered. For example, square, rectangular, irregular, or pie-shaped. If the shape adversely affects the value of the subject property, then comments should be made here or in the additional comments section.

View   The view from within the subject property is entered. Obstructed views may or may not adversely affect the value of the property. Conversely, views of mountains, water, or nature preserves may be more desirable, which translates into a higher property value. As with all elements of comparison, the impact on the value of the subject depends upon the views of comparable properties within the market.

Specific Zoning Classification   The specific zoning classification of the subject property assigned by the local zoning authority is entered here (e.g., R-3 Multiple Family Residential). The zoning classification indicates the permitted property use(s). If the property is located within an area that is not zoned, then N/A is entered.

Zoning Description   Enter any additional comments that may be needed to describe the zoning classification.

Zoning Compliance   The appraiser determines if the use of the subject is a permitted use within the specific zoning classification. Once this is determined, the proper box is checked indicating legal, legal nonconforming (grandfathered use), no zoning, or illegal. If the property use is a legal nonconforming use, it may be necessary to comment on any adverse affect to the property value as a result of this current property use. If the no zoning box is checked, the appraiser must determine if the subject use is restricted by other private restrictions such as deed restrictions. If the illegal box is checked, this indicates that the subject use has not been permitted by either a variance or special use permit. If this is the case, additional explanation is needed.

Is the highest and best use of the subject property as improved (or as proposed per plans and specifications) the present use?   The appraiser determines if the current or proposed use of the subject property is the highest and best use of the property as if improved. If the no box is checked, further explanation is needed to describe the use of the property that is the highest and best use as improved.

Utilities   Utilities available to the subject as well as the sources of these utilities are indicated. If the other box is checked, then ownership of this utility should be indicated, as well as the acceptance in the market. For example, the source of the sanitary sewer may be a septic system.

Off-site Improvements—Type   In this area the material composition of the street and the alley is indicated. Also, whether the street and alley is privately maintained or maintained at the expense of the public is indicated. If there is no alley, then none is indicated.

FEMA Special Flood Hazard Area   Flood hazard areas are identified throughout the United States by the Federal Emergency Management Agency (FEMA). The appraiser checks published maps to determine if any part of the subject is located in a designated flood hazard area and indicates by checking the yes or no box. If only part of the site is located in a flood hazard area but improvements are not located in a flood hazard area, the yes box is checked and additional comments are needed in the additional comments section. It is important that the appraiser checks the most recent and updated flood maps.

FEMA Flood Zone   If the appraiser determines that any part of the subject site is located in a designated flood hazard area, the specified flood zone is indicated.

FEMA Map Number   If the appraiser determines that any part of the subject site is located in a designated flood hazard area, the map panel number is indicated.

FEMA Map Date   If the appraiser determines that any part of the subject site is located in a designated flood hazard area, the map date is indicated.

Are the utilities and off-site improvements typical for the market area?   The appraiser determines if the utilities and off-site improvements of the subject property are typical for the neighborhood. If not, then explanation is needed. Since space is limited, additional comments can be placed in the additional comments section.

Are there any adverse site conditions or external factors (easements, encroachments, environmental conditions, land uses, etc.)?   Any visible easements besides those indicated on a plat of survey are described here. Usually residential properties will have public utility easements, shared driveways, subsurface water and gas line easements, and telephone and electrical wires overhead. The contour of the land (topography) is also reported here, for example sloping or level. If the topography of the subject property does not conform, resulting in an adverse affect on the subject's property value, then additional explanation is needed.

IMPROVEMENTS SECTION

General Description	Foundation	Exterior Description materials/condition	Interior materials/condition
Units ☐ One ☐ One with Accessory Unit	☐ Concrete Slab ☐ Crawl Space	Foundation Walls	Floors
# of Stories	☐ Full Basement ☐ Partial Basement	Exterior Walls	Walls
Type ☐ Det. ☐ Att. ☐ S-Det./End Unit	Basement Area sq. ft.	Roof Surface	Trim/Finish
☐ Existing ☐ Proposed ☐ Under Const.	Basement Finish %	Gutters & Downspouts	Bath Floor
Design (Style)	☐ Outside Entry/Exit ☐ Sump Pump	Window Type	Bath Wainscot
Year Built	Evidence of ☐ Infestation	Storm Sash/Insulated	Car Storage ☐ None
Effective Age (Yrs)	☐ Dampness ☐ Settlement	Screens	☐ Driveway # of Cars
Attic ☐ None	Heating ☐ FWA ☐ HWBB ☐ Radiant	Amenities ☐ Woodstove(s) #	Driveway Surface
☐ Drop Stair ☐ Stairs	☐ Other Fuel	☐ Fireplace(s) # ☐ Fence	☐ Garage # of Cars
☐ Floor ☐ Scuttle	Cooling ☐ Central Air Conditioning	☐ Patio/Deck ☐ Porch	☐ Carport # of Cars
☐ Finished ☐ Heated	☐ Individual ☐ Other	☐ Pool ☐ Other	☐ Att. ☐ Det. ☐ Built-in
Appliances ☐Refrigerator ☐Range/Oven ☐Dishwasher ☐Disposal ☐Microwave ☐Washer/Dryer ☐Other (describe)			
Finished area **above** grade contains: Rooms Bedrooms Bath(s) Square Feet of Gross Living Area Above Grade			
Additional features (special energy efficient items, etc.)			
Describe the condition of the property (including needed repairs, deterioration, renovations, remodeling, etc.).			
Are there any physical deficiencies or adverse conditions that affect the livability, soundness, or structural integrity of the property? ☐ Yes ☐ No If Yes, describe			
Does the property generally conform to the neighborhood (functional utility, style, condition, use, construction, etc.)? ☐ Yes ☐ No If No, describe			

General Description   The appraiser checks the appropriate box that describes the subject, indicating the number of units, the number of stories, if subject is attached or detached, whether or not the subject is existing, proposed, or under construction, the design style, the year built, and the effective age.

Foundation   The appraiser indicates the type of foundation, whether there is a full or partial basement, the size of the basement, and the percentage of the basement that is finished. If there is an outside entrance to the basement, whether there is a sump pump, and evidence of insect infestation, dampness, or settlement is also indicated. Insect infestation, a damp basement, and/or foundation settlement can adversely affect the value of the subject property. The cost to cure these deficiencies, if they are curable, may need to be addressed. Additional explanation is needed in the additional comments section.

Exterior Description Materials/Condition   The material composition and the condition of the foundation walls, the exterior walls, the roof surface, and the gutter downspouts are indicated here. For example, for foundation walls, the appraiser would write "concrete block/good." The window type and information about the storm sash (storm windows) and screens is indicated. If not all of the windows have a storm window or screen, then entering partial is appropriate.

Interior Materials/Condition   The material composition and the condition of the floor, walls, trim work, bathroom floor, and bathroom wainscot is indicated. For example, if the floor covering throughout the home is part carpet, part ceramic, and part hardwood, the floor could be described as "crpt/cer/hw." Condition identifiers such as "poor," "average," and "good" are used to denote the condition.

Attic   If the subject does not have an attic, then the "None" box is checked. If the subject does have an attic, then the type of access and whether the attic has a floor or is heated and/or finished is indicated by checking the proper box or boxes.

Heating   The appraiser indicates whether the subject is heated by forced warm air, hot water baseboard, or radiant heat. The other box is checked for some other form of heating, such as solar or space heating.

Fuel   The appraiser indicates how the heating system is fueled, for example, gas, oil, electricity, or coal.

Cooling   The appraiser indicates whether the subject is heated by central air-conditioning, individual window units, or units mounted into wall sleeves. The other box is checked for some other form of cooling, such as an evaporative cooler.

Amenities   The appraiser indicates whether the subject has a woodstove or a fireplace and the number of such amenities is indicated. If the subject has a fence, a patio or deck, a porch, or a swimming pool it is indicated by checking the appropriate box or boxes. The other box is checked if the subject has an amenity not listed, such as a screened-in gazebo or storage shed.

Car Storage   The appraiser checks the appropriate box indicating whether the subject has car storage. If not, then the "None" box is checked. If the subject has a driveway then the number of cars that can be parked legally in the driveway is indicated.

Driveway Surface   The appraiser indicates the type of surface (paving) of the driveway. If the subject does not have a driveway, then N/A is indicated. The type of driveway surface is indicated by entering concrete, gravel, asphalt, or stones.

Garage   The appraiser indicates whether the subject has a garage and, if so, the number of cars that can be stored in it.

Carport   The appraiser indicates whether the subject has a carport and, if so, the number of cars that can be stored in it.

Attached (Att.)   If the garage shares one common wall with the home, then this box is checked.

Detached (Det.)   If the garage does not share a common wall with the home, then this box is checked.

Built-in   If the garage shares a common wall with the home and the second floor of the home extends over the garage, then this box is checked.

Appliances   The appraiser indicates built in appliances that are considered to be fixtures within the home. The other box is checked if the home has an appliance such as a free-standing freezer. Free-standing appliances are considered personal property and should not be included in the value of the real estate.

Finished area above grade contains   The appraiser indicates the number of rooms, bedrooms, bath(s), and the square footage of gross living area above grade. Rooms that are not typically included in the room count include foyers and utility rooms. Areas that are below the exterior grade are considered to be below grade. Most basements, finished or not, are not to be included in the square footage of the gross living area. Split-level homes with a finished lower level that is not completely below grade are still not to be included in the square footage of gross living area above grade. Attic space can be included in gross living area and room count if the area is heated, finished similar to other areas of the home, has adequate fenestration (window and door openings) similar to the remaining areas of the home, and the average ceiling height (considering sloping roof lines) is 7 feet or higher.

Additional features (special energy efficient items, etc.)   This area is used to indicate features not previously provided for. Such features include skylights, hot tubs, green houses, security systems, underground sprinkling systems, wet bars, solar heating systems, and high-efficiency furnaces.

Describe the condition of the property (including needed repairs, deterioration, renovations, remodeling, etc.).   The appraiser indicates any observed physical deterioration that is above and beyond what is expected considering the age and quality of construction. Functional obsolescence resulting in a negative market response to either a super improvement (super adequacy) or a poor floor plan is also reported. External obsolescence due to factors outside the subject property lines is indicated. For example, the home's proximity to a landfill or an area that has excessive noise and/or traffic.

Improvements and renovations are also reported, for example, a room addition or a new roof. For consistency, these physical, functional, and external factors should be accounted for in the cost approach section.

Are there any physical deficiencies or adverse conditions that affect the livability, soundness, or structural integrity of the property?   During the course of the appraisal if the appraiser observes or becomes aware of any adverse environmental conditions, such as hazardous wastes, such conditions must be reported. The appraiser must check the appropriate box and comment on the effects that any uncovered conditions have on the market value of the subject.

Does the property generally conform to the neighborhood (functional utility, style, condition, use, construction, etc.)?   After the appraiser determines if the subject property generally conforms to the neighborhood, the proper box is checked. The principle of conformity and progression/regression are discussed here. For example, if the subject is the "white elephant" of the neighborhood, then the principle of regression dictates that the market value of the subject will be adversely affected by the surrounding properties. In this case, the no box is checked and the appraiser must explain.

LESSON 2 REVIEW QUESTIONS

1. The subject must be identified is such a way that it can easily be _____.

2. For properties that are located outside of city limits, the city of the _____ serving the subject can be indicated.

3. The person acquiring the funds from the lender/client is the _____.

4. _____ tract data provides population and housing statistics for a specific area.

5. _____ assessments are assessments levied against the subject property for roads or sewer.

6. A clubhouse, swimming pool, green belt, and security posts are all examples of common areas within a(n) _____.

7. A purchase transaction or a refinance transaction is considered to be the _____ of the appraisal assignment.

8. An important indicator of the market's acceptance of a particular property is the _____ the property is offered for sale prior to a contract sale as well as any large _____ between the asking price and the contract price.

9. Lenders, sellers, buyers, and sales brokers are all examples of _____.

10. The appraiser determines if the subject property is located in a(n) _____, _____, or _____ area, and checks the proper box.

11. The location, the percentage built-up, and growth are located in the _____ section.

12. To determine demand and supply, the appraiser checks the _____ of properties within the subject neighborhood.

13. If there is a relatively low marketing time, then it can be assumed that there is a potential for _____ demand than supply, thus a(n) _____ of one-unit housing.

14. Under-priced housing will sell _____ than over-priced housing.

15. The appraiser determines the range of sales prices within the subject neighborhood and eliminates the _____ low and the _____ high sales price in the range of sales prices.

16. Neighborhood boundaries should correspond with the _____ exhibit attached to the report.

17. Employment stability, convenience to employment, convenience to school, and convenience to shopping are features that are commented on in the _____ description area.

18. The availability of financing and apparent trends are factors of market _____.

19. Above market interest rates will result in _____ sales prices.

20. Concrete slab, crawl space, full basement, partial basement are all identified in the _____ section.

LESSON 2 REVIEW ANSWERS

1. located

2. post office

3. borrower

4. Census

5. Special

6. PUD

7. purpose

8. length of time; differences/discrepancies

9. data sources

10. urban; suburban; rural

11. neighborhood

12. marketing time

13. greater; shortage

14. faster

15. extreme; extreme

16. map

17. neighborhood

18. conditions

19. lower

20. improvements

LESSON 3: The URAR, Pages 2 and 3

SALES COMPARISON APPROACH SECTION

There are	comparable properties currently offered for sale in the subject neighborhood ranging in price from $				to $		
There are	comparable sales in the subject neighborhood within the past twelve months ranging in sale price from $				to $		

FEATURE	SUBJECT	COMPARABLE SALE # 1		COMPARABLE SALE # 2		COMPARABLE SALE # 3	
Address							
Proximity to Subject							
Sale Price	$		$		$		$
Sale Price/Gross Liv. Area	$ sq. ft.	$ sq. ft.		$ sq. ft.		$ sq. ft.	
Data Source(s)							
Verification Source(s)							
VALUE ADJUSTMENTS	DESCRIPTION	DESCRIPTION	+(-) $ Adjustment	DESCRIPTION	+(-) $ Adjustment	DESCRIPTION	+(-) $ Adjustment
Sale or Financing Concessions							
Date of Sale/Time							
Location							
Leasehold/Fee Simple							
Site							
View							
Design (Style)							
Quality of Construction							
Actual Age							
Condition							
Above Grade	Total Bdrms. Baths	Total Bdrms. Baths		Total Bdrms. Baths		Total Bdrms. Baths	
Room Count							
Gross Living Area	sq. ft.	sq. ft.		sq. ft.		sq. ft.	
Basement & Finished Rooms Below Grade							
Functional Utility							
Heating/Cooling							
Energy Efficient Items							
Garage/Carport							
Porch/Patio/Deck							
Net Adjustment (Total)		☐ + ☐ -	$	☐ + ☐ -	$	☐ + ☐ -	$
Adjusted Sale Price of Comparables		Net Adj. % Gross Adj. %	$	Net Adj. % Gross Adj. %	$	Net Adj. % Gross Adj. %	$

I ☐ did ☐ did not research the sale or transfer history of the subject property and comparable sales. If not, explain

My research ☐ did ☐ did not reveal any prior sales or transfers of the subject property for the three years prior to the effective date of this appraisal.

Data source(s)

My research ☐ did ☐ did not reveal any prior sales or transfers of the comparable sales for the year prior to the date of sale of the comparable sale.

Data source(s)

Report the results of the research and analysis of the prior sale or transfer history of the subject property and comparable sales (report additional prior sales on page 3).

ITEM	SUBJECT	COMPARABLE SALE # 1	COMPARABLE SALE # 2	COMPARABLE SALE # 3
Date of Prior Sale/Transfer				
Price of Prior Sale/Transfer				
Data Source(s)				
Effective Date of Data Source(s)				

Analysis of prior sale or transfer history of the subject property and comparable sales

Summary of Sales Comparison Approach

Indicated Value by Sales Comparison Approach $

If the subject is located in an active market, then information on comparable properties will be plentiful. The appraiser must use the skills he or she has acquired to determine which properties are indeed comparable to the subject. Information is indicated on comparables currently offered for sale and on comparables that have sold during the past 12 months.

The methodized process under the sales comparison approach is as follows:

1. Research the relevant sales data collected from the market

2. Verify data and validity of arm's-length transaction

3. Choose the units of comparison that are relevant

4. Adjust for differences in elements of comparison

5. Reconcile to value indication under the sales comparison approach

What determines relevance of data is the applicability of the information when compared with the market and the subject property. The subject has features and characteristics that are likely to have value in the marketplace. To determine the value, similar properties that have transacted at a known sales price from the market are compared to the subject. The comparable sale must be arm's-length and verified as a market transaction if market value is to be sought. Within a specific market the appraiser must analyze information gathered during the general data collection process and determine which unit or units of comparison accurately depict the expectations of the market participants. The comparable properties are compared to the subject and the differences are accounted for in the sales grid as adjustments. An indicated value for each comparable sale is then rendered.

Adjustments are derived by performing a paired sales analysis, also referred to as paired data analysis or matched pairs analysis, whereby the differences are isolated between other recently sold properties, and a quantitative or qualitative adjustment is applied to the comparable where there is a difference from the subject. These differences result in either a positive or a negative adjustment. The important point to remember is that the *comparable adjusts to the subject*. Therefore, if the comparable is *superior to the subject* the adjustment must be *negative* to make the comparable similar to the subject. Conversely, if the comparable is *inferior to the subject* a *positive* adjustment must be made to the comparable sales price to make the comparable similar to the subject.

Feature   Elements of comparison that will be adjusted for any differences when compared to the subject.

Subject   Elements are entered in this column for the subject. This information was collected during the specific data collection part of the appraisal process.

Comparable Sales #1, Comparable Sales #2, Comparable Sales #3   Elements are entered in these three columns for the three comparable sales. While only three sales are entered on the URAR, the appraiser analyzes data collected from other sales as well. After a complete analysis of comparable sales, the appraiser chooses the three that are the most comparable to the subject and are the best indicators of value.

Address   The same address entered in the Subject section is entered. Addresses are also entered for comparable sales #1, #2, and #3.

Proximity to Subject   The distance in terms of blocks, miles, or fractions of miles and the direction (north, south, east, west) from the subject is entered for each comparable. For example, "1/2 block south" or "1/4 mile northeast."

Sales Price   The current contract sales price for the subject and the comparables is entered. If the subject has not been sold, then N/A is entered.

Sales Price/Gross Living Area   The sales price per gross living area (GLA) is entered. This is calculated by dividing the sales price by the square footage of above grade living area. For example, if the sales price is $320,000 and the gross living area is 2,500 square feet, $128 would be entered ($320,000 ÷ 2,500).

Data Source(s)   The source or sources of market data collected is entered. Examples of sources include, but are not limited to, personal inspection, broker, lender, seller, public records, and multiple listing services (MLSs).

Verification Source(s)   The source or sources that verified the data is entered. Examples include, but are not limited to, appraiser's files, county recorder's records, MLSs, and lenders.

Value Adjustments   All adjustments, using the adjustment process discussed earlier, made in the grid must be supported by the market. These adjustments are entered as dollars in the column next to the description of the element that is being compared to the subject.

Sales or Financing Concessions   Implicit in the definition of market value is that payments to the seller are made in terms of cash or cash equivalency and that the property is unaffected by special or creative financing or sales concessions. If a comparable sale involved special sales or financing concessions you must make adjustments—whether positive or negative. Seller financing with terms and conditions different from what is offered in the financing market, special loan types, and usual terms of a loan are all examples of special sales or financing concessions.

Cash equivalency is the adjustment made to the comparable sales price if it was sold with atypical financing. For example, the sales price of a comparable sale that reflects a premium paid for the benefit of receiving seller financing is needed to determine the present value of property. This cash equivalency adjustment, which is calculated from the buyer's point of view rather than the lender's point of view, can either be made in the sales comparison approach by paired sales analysis or in the income approach. Generally speaking, if the market supplies an abundance of comparable data, then these comparable sales with the various issues mentioned should be omitted.

Date of Sale/Time   The closing date of the sales is indicated, as well as any adjustment for market conditions (time). Because the principle of change dictates that nothing remains static and that everything changes over time, the date that a sale occurred is extremely important. The greater the difference between the effective date of an appraisal and the sale date of the comparable sale, the greater the potential for significant impacts on value. However, even if a short time has transpired since the comparable sale date and the effective date, a major change on the market economic base can significantly impact values in that market. For example, a recent comparable sale, two months prior to the effective date, may need to be adjusted for market conditions. An adjustment may be needed because it was just announced that a large manufacturing plant in the immediate area will be closing. Property values can be significantly impacted due to large layoffs and the subsequent market reaction to the forces that affect value. Likewise, property values can be significantly enhanced by the arrival of a new airport or large business, thus creating new employment opportunities.

Location   The location subject is rated, and a rating of good, average, or poor is indicated. The location of each comparable sale is than rated relative to the subject's location, and a rating of superior, equal, or inferior is indicated. Under ideal circumstances, the subject and all comparable sales would be located within the same neighborhood. However, this is not always possible; therefore, any differences in location, even within the same neighborhood, must be accounted for.

Leasehold/Fee Simple   The form of ownership for the subject is the same as reported in the subject section on the previous page of the URAR. Comparable sales must be adjusted for differences in property rights conveyed. For example, if the property rights conveyed for the subject is a leasehold interest, the owner of a comparable sale might have a fee simple estate. These differences can have a significant impact on property value. The ownership rights for one-unit properties are typically fee simple.

Site   The size of the subject site is indicated and should be the same as reported on the previous page of the URAR. The site size of each comparable sale is then compared to the subject and a rating of superior, equal, or inferior is indicated. Adjustments, if necessary, are indicated for size, shape, topography, and so on.

View   An abbreviated description as well as a rating of good, average, or poor for both the subject and the comparables is indicated. For example, "wtr/gd" may be used to describe a water view that is rated as good. Adjustments, if necessary, are indicated.

Design (Style)   The architectural design of subject is identified and a rating of good, average, or poor is indicated. The architectural design of each comparable sale is identified and then rated relative to the subject. A rating of superior, equal, or inferior is indicated. Adjustments, if necessary, are indicated.

Quality of Construction   The quality of construction of the subject is identified and a rating of good, average, or poor is indicated. The architectural design of each comparable sale is identified and then rated relative to the subject, A rating of superior, equal, or inferior is indicated. Adjustments, if necessary, are indicated.

Actual Age   The actual (physical or chronological) age of the subject of each comparable is indicated. Ideally, comparables that are similar in age are used, and no adjustments are necessary.

Condition   The condition of the subject is identified and a rating of good, average, or poor is indicated. The condition of each comparable sale is identified and then rated relative to the subject and a rating of superior, equal, or inferior is indicated. Adjustments, if necessary, are indicated.

Above Grade Room Count/Gross Living Area   The number of above grade rooms, bedrooms, and bathrooms for both the subject and comparable sales are indicated. Adjustments, if necessary, are indicated.

Basement and Finished Rooms Below Grade   Enter the requested information about the basement for the subject and the comparables. Indicate whether the basement is full or partial, the percentage or square footage of finished space, and identify the type of rooms. For example, "full, 50%, den." Adjustments, if necessary, are indicated.

Functional Utility   A rating of good, average, or poor for both the subject and the comparables is indicated. It is important to note that adjustments are made only if the market's response to the functional utility dictates such a change.

Heating/Cooling The types of heating and cooling systems for both the subject and the comparables are indicated. Adjustments, if necessary, are indicated.

Energy Efficient Items Energy efficient items such as solar-heating systems are identified for subject and comparables. Adjustments, if necessary, are indicated.

Garage/Carport Garage and/or carport information for the subject and comparables is indicated. Adjustments, if necessary, are indicated.

Porch/Patio/Deck Porch, patio, or deck information for the subject and comparables is indicated. Adjustments, if necessary, are indicated. Additional lines are available to identify and adjust for the fences, swimming pools, gazebos, and so on.

Net Adjustment (Total) The net adjustment for each comparable sale is calculated and entered. A net adjustment is then the sum of all positive and negative adjustments. A shortcoming of net adjustments is that a series of net adjustments can potentially zero each other out.

Adjusted Sales Price of Comparables The lump-sum dollar adjustments within each sale are then netted out and the net result is either added or subtracted from the sales price to reach an indicated value for each comparable.

Net Adj. Percent (%) The net adjustment percentage is calculated by dividing the total net adjustment dollar amount by the sales price.

Gross Adj. Percent (%) A gross adjustment is the result of adding all of the adjustments for a comparable and ignoring the signs. In other words, it is the total dollar amount of adjustments ignoring whether the adjustment is negative or positive. Gross adjustments indicate whether a comparable sale is reliable. The comparable with the least amount of gross adjustments is usually the most reliable indicator of subject value. To calculate the gross adjustment percentage, divide the total gross adjustment dollar amount by the sales price.

I did or did not research the sale or transfer history of the subject property and comparable sales. If not, explain. The proper box is checked indicating whether the appraiser researched the sale or transfer history of the subject and comparable sales. Further explanation is needed if the Did Not box was checked.

My research did or did not reveal any prior sales or transfers of the subject property for the three years prior to the effective date of this report. The proper box is checked indicating whether there were any prior sales or transfers.

Data Source(s)   The source of the subject sales history information is identified.

My research did or did not reveal any prior sales or transfers of the comparable sales for the year prior to the date of sale of the comparable sale.   The proper box is checked indicating whether there were any prior sales or transfers.

Data Source(s)   The source of the sales history information of the comparables is identified.

Report the results of the research and analysis of the prior sale or transfer history of the subject and comparable sales (report additional prior sales on page 3).   The prior sale or transfer information, including dates and dollar amounts, data sources, and the effective date of the data sources is entered in the grid below this statement.

Analysis of prior sale or transfer history of the subject property and comparable sales.   The information that was collected is analyzed and summarized.

Summary of Sales Comparison Approach   The reconciliation process within the sales comparison approach is summarized here. The appraiser can identify which comparable was considered to be the most reliable indicator of value for the subject and why.

Indicated Value of Sales Comparison Approach   The appraiser's value opinion (in dollars) using the sales comparison approach is indicated.

RECONCILIATION SECTION

Indicated Value by: Sales Comparison Approach $	Cost Approach (if developed) $	Income Approach (if developed) $

This appraisal is made ☐ "as is", ☐ subject to completion per plans and specifications on the basis of a hypothetical condition that the improvements have been completed, ☐ subject to the following repairs or alterations on the basis of a hypothetical condition that the repairs or alterations have been completed, or ☐ subject to the following required inspection based on the extraordinary assumption that the condition or deficiency does not require alteration or repair:

Based on a complete visual inspection of the interior and exterior areas of the subject property, defined scope of work, statement of assumptions and limiting conditions, and appraiser's certification, my (our) opinion of the market value, as defined, of the real property that is the subject of this report is
$, as of   , which is the date of inspection and the effective date of this appraisal.

Reconciliation is the last step in the development aspect of the appraisal process. There are actually several places in which reconciliation takes place. Reconciliation takes place at the end of each approach to value and then at the end of the development phase of the appraisal process, but before reporting. The reconciliation that takes place at the end of the development aspect of the appraisal process, sometimes called the overall reconciliation, is concerned with the conclusion that has the most validity and is the most appropriate to solve the original problem. It is critical for reconciliation to take place at the end of each approach. This is for the benefit of accurately reaching conclusions within the approach using critical thinking. Then the indicated value by the approach is submitted for consideration where the strengths and weaknesses of the approach and conclusions are carefully considered during the final reconciliation and the overall value conclusion.

Indicated Value By   After reconciliation within each approach, the indicated values for each approach are entered. The indicated values by each approach and the strengths and weaknesses of each approach are considered and summarized.

This appraisal is made as is.   This box is checked for an existing property.

This appraisal is made subject to completion per plans and specifications...   This box is checked if the subject property is proposed new construction or under construction.

This appraisal is made subject to the following repairs or alterations...   This box is checked if the appraiser identified curable physical deficiencies or conditions that affect safeness and soundness of the structure. The final value conclusion that the appraiser attests to assumes that these deficiencies will be cured/corrected.

This appraisal is made subject to the following required inspection...   This box is checked if the appraiser identified the need for an inspection (by a trained professional) for curable physical deficiencies or conditions that affect safeness and soundness of the structure. The final value conclusion that the appraiser attests to assumes that these deficiencies or conditions will be cured/corrected.

Based on a complete visual inspection of the interior and exterior.   The final value conclusion in dollars and the effective date of the appraisal are indicated.

ADDITIONAL COMMENTS SECTION

This section is used for any additional comments or explanations that do not fit within the various sections of the URAR. If this space does not provide for all of the additional comments, then an addendum can be added to the report.

COST APPROACH SECTION

COST APPROACH TO VALUE (not required by Fannie Mae)				
Provide adequate information for the lender/client to replicate the below cost figures and calculations.				
Support for the opinion of site value (summary of comparable land sales or other methods for estimating site value)				
ESTIMATED ☐ REPRODUCTION OR ☐ REPLACEMENT COST NEW	OPINION OF SITE VALUE .... = $			
Source of cost data	Dwelling	Sq. Ft. @ $	.... =$	
Quality rating from cost service Effective date of cost data		Sq. Ft. @ $	.... =$	
Comments on Cost Approach (gross living area calculations, depreciation, etc.)				
	Garage/Carport	Sq. Ft. @ $	.... =$	
	Total Estimate of Cost-New		.... = $	
	Less	Physical	Functional	External
	Depreciation			=$( )
	Depreciated Cost of Improvements....................................... =$			
	"As-is" Value of Site Improvements....................................... =$			
Estimated Remaining Economic Life (HUD and VA only) Years	Indicated Value By Cost Approach .... =$			

The cost approach is a methodized process to derive a value indication whereby the *replacement cost* or the *reproduction cost* of a building is first estimated including the entrepreneurial profit, then accrued depreciation is subtracted, and finally the value of the land or site as though vacant is added to conclude a value indication using the cost approach.

Replacement or reproduction cost new (RCN)

– Accrued depreciation

= Depreciated cost of the improvements

+ Land (site) value as though vacant

= Indicated value using the cost approach

The applicability of the cost approach is founded in the principle of substitution as mentioned under Related Principles. Remember that the principle of substitution related to the cost approach stated that "no person is justified paying more for a property than they could build new without undue delay." The implication of the related principle of substitution is that market value and the cost of the property are closely related with newer properties. This leads to the concept that the cost approach is likely to be most applicable in newly constructed or relatively new properties. In theory, the market is likely to be knowledgeable about the forces that affect and create value and therefore the property would not be built if the cost to build was not feasible. Given that the land value is well-supported and that the costs associated with the construction of the property are similar to the current cost new with little or no accrued depreciation, the cost approach has substantial validity as an indicator of value.

The cost approach also is useful for determining market value in situations where the sales comparison and income approaches lack validity or applicability. For example, in single-family valuation the income approach may not have validity in a market where the income stream associated with the ownership of property does not drive ownership of the property and the market might lack recent or comparable sales that would support a value conclusion under the sales comparison approach. Likewise, if the property has a low effective age and, therefore, little physical depreciation with identifiable or little obsolescence, then the cost approach is likely to be representative of the market value of the property.

Important note: Fannie Mae does not require the appraiser to report the cost approach to value and they do not accept appraisals that rely solely upon the cost approach to arrive a final value indicator.

Support for the opinion of site value (summary of comparable land sales or other methods of estimating site value)   The appraiser describes the method used to derive to the opinion of site value if a method was used other than the sales comparison method. Further details are provided including availability of market data, adjustments to comparables, etc.

Estimated Reproduction or Replacement Cost New   The proper box is checked indicating whether reproduction costs or replacement costs were used.

Source of cost data   The source(s) for the cost estimation is indicated. For example, area builders, suppliers, and contractors or a cost-estimating service such as Marshall & Swift.

Quality rating from cost service   The quality rating provided by the cost estimating service is indicated.

Effective date of cost data   The effective date of cost data used in the cost estimate is indicated.

Comments on Cost Approach (gross living area calculations, depreciation, etc.)   If the appraiser determines that the subject suffers from physical depreciation beyond what is expected considering the effective age of the property, explanations are provided in this space. If functional and/or external obsolescence exist, explanation is provided here.

Estimated Remaining Economic Life (HUD and VA only)   The remaining economic life (REL) is the time that the existing improvements are likely to contribute economically to the value of the property. HUD and VA require this to be entered and expressed in years.

Opinion of Site Value ($) The appraiser's opinion of site value is entered.

Dwelling The square footage of the dwelling and any other component such as a basement or a porch is listed, along with the estimated cost new per square foot. The square footage is then multiplied by the cost new per square foot and the result is indicated. Extra lines are provided for special energy efficient items such as a solar heating system.

Garage/Carport The square footage of the garage or carport is listed along with the estimated cost new per square foot. The square footage is then multiplied by the cost new per square foot and the result is indicated.

Total Estimate of Cost New The total dollar amounts, with the exception of site value, are added, resulting in a total estimate of cost new.

Less Depreciation—Physical, Functional, External Accrued depreciation is the total loss in value from all causes: physical, functional, and external. Physical depreciation is the loss in value as a result of general wear and tear. Obsolescence is the negative market-response to an item. There are two types of obsolescence: functional obsolescence and external obsolescence. Functional obsolescence is a value loss as a result of the market's negative response to some functionality of the property, such as a poor floor plan. Sometimes there may be a loss in value as a result of an over-improvement. This is a functional obsolescence that results in a superadequacy. In such cases, the market will not pay the additional costs associated with the item. For example, high-quality gold plumbing fixtures in a tract home would be extravagant items for which the market would not likely pay additional funds. *External obsolescence* is a value loss realized as a result of the market's negative response to something that is outside of the property lines. External obsolescence is never curable, as the ability to rectify the issue is beyond the control of the property owner. The most challenging aspect of the cost approach is the depreciation calculation. The appraiser indicates the depreciation from all causes, if present, as a percentage. The percentage is then multiplied by the total estimate of cost new to arrive at a depreciation dollar amount.

Depreciated Cost of Improvements The total depreciation amount is subtracted from the total estimate of cost new.

"As-is" Value of Site Improvements The value of items such as sidewalks, driveways, or landscaping, in their current condition that were not considered in the opinion of site value are indicated.

Indicated Value by Cost Approach The summation of the opinion of site value, the depreciated cost of improvements, and the as-is value of site improvements is entered.

INCOME SECTION

INCOME APPROACH TO VALUE (not required by Fannie Mae)				
Estimated Monthly Market Rent $	X Gross Rent Multiplier	= $	Indicated Value by Income Approach	
Summary of Income Approach (including support for market rent and GRM)				

The *income approach* to value has within it several methods of determining value based on the property's ability to create and maintain an income stream. The major premise behind the income approach is that the future benefits of the income stream have value in the present time. The income approach is generally used with income-producing properties, such as apartment buildings (5+ units), office/retail buildings, and shopping centers; however, it is also used for small residential income producing properties (1–4 units), vacant land, and single-family homes. The price that a buyer should be expected to pay for a property should be reflective of the expected income level that the property will produce. The more income that a property produces the greater the return on the investment for the buyer. Therefore, the more desirable the property is, the greater the price that the property is likely to command.

Income capitalization is a process to convert income to value. For single-family homes, the income is in the form of monthly market rent. The income is then capitalized using a multiple derived from the market. For single-family residential properties, a gross rent multiplier (GRM) is used. A multiplier is the result after dividing the sales price (value) by the monthly rent. Gross income multipliers are extracted from comparable sales in the market by dividing the value (sales price) by the monthly rent. The multiplier is then multiplied by the monthly rent of the subject resulting in an estimated value for the subject. The formula can be expressed as:

$$GRM (M) = Value (V) \div Gross\ rent (I)$$

For example, consider the following information that was collected from the market:

Sale Number	Gross Rent	Value	GRM (value ÷ gross rent)
1	$1,800	$300,000	167
2	$1,750	$288,750	165
3	$1,760	$290,400	165
4	$1,725	$284,625	165

If all four comparables are considered similar to the subject, then based on the range of multipliers indicated above, the appraiser may reconcile to 165. If the subject has a market rent of $1,745, the indicated value of the subject is estimated at $287,925 ($1,745 × 165).

Estimated monthly market rent $ ________ × Gross rent multiplier = ________$ __________ Indicated value by the income approach

The estimated monthly rent for the subject is entered and multiplied by the appropriate GRM obtained from the market, resulting in the indicated value by the income approach to value.

Summary of Income Approach (including support for market rent and GRM) The basis for the appraiser's conclusions is provided here. The reasoning and support used to derive market rent for the subject, as well as extraction of the gross rent multiplier, are included.

PUD SECTION

PUD INFORMATION	PROJECT INFORMATION FOR PUDs (if applicable)		
	Is the developer/builder in control of the Homeowners' Association (HOA)? ☐ Yes ☐ No Unit type(s) ☐ Detached ☐ Attached		
	Provide the following information for PUDs ONLY if the developer/builder is in control of the HOA and the subject property is an attached dwelling unit.		
	Legal name of project		
	Total number of phases	Total number of units	Total number of units sold
	Total number of units rented	Total number of units for sale	Data source(s)
	Was the project created by the conversion of an existing building(s) into a PUD? ☐ Yes ☐ No If Yes, date of conversion		
	Does the project contain any multi-dwelling units? ☐ Yes ☐ No Data source(s)		
	Are the units, common elements, and recreation facilities complete? ☐ Yes ☐ No If No, describe the status of completion.		
	Are the common elements leased to or by the Homeowners' Association? ☐ Yes ☐ No If Yes, describe the rental terms and options.		
	Describe common elements and recreational facilities		

Is the developer/builder in control of the Homeowners' Association (HOA)? Although local laws vary from state to state, when a PUD is established the builder is in control of the homeowners' association until a specific percentage of units are sold. Once a certain number of units have sold, the homeowners can take control of the HOA. The proper box is checked indicating if the developer is in control of the HOA.

Unit type(s) The proper box is checked indicating if the subject is a detached or attached dwelling unit.

Provide the following information for PUDs ONLY if the developer/builder is in control of the HOA and the subject property is an attached dwelling unit. The appraiser needs to fill out the remaining PUD information if the subject is a detached dwelling unit.

Legal name of project The legal name of the project is indicated.

Total number of phases   Usually PUDs are built over a period of time in phases. The number of phases is indicated.

Total number of units   The total number of individual units, which can be town homes, detached single-family homes, or condominiums in the PUD, is indicated.

Total number of units sold   The number of units within the PUD that were sold as of the effective date of the appraisal is indicated.

Total number of units rented   The total number of non-owner-occupied units is indicated.

Total number of units for sale   The number of units currently offered for sale is indicated.

Data source(s)   The data source(s) is indicated. Sources include lenders, the HOA, the builder/developer, the unit owner, and so on.

Was the project created by the conversion of an existing building(s) into a PUD? If Yes, date of conversion.   The appropriate box is checked indicating if the project is a conversion. If the yes box is checked, the date of conversion is indicated. If the project is a recent conversion, a higher number of currently offered for sale and a lesser number of units sold will be reasonable.

Does the project contain any multi-dwelling units? Data source(s)   The appropriate box is checked indicating if the PUD has multidwelling units. The data sources(s) are indicated. Sources include lenders, the HOA, the builder/developer, the unit owner, and so on.

Are the units, common elements, and recreation facilities complete? If No, describe the status of completion.   The appropriate box is checked, if the no box is checked further explanation on the status of completion is needed. Generally, the builder/developer is required to set aside funds for the completion of all common elements.

Are the common elements leased to or by the Homeowners' Association? If Yes, describe the rental terms and options.   The proper box is checked indicating if the common elements are leased. If the yes box is checked, the terms and conditions of the arrangement are analyzed and explained.

Describe common elements and recreational facilities   Common elements include greenbelt maintenance, entrance security guards, and subdivision entrance signs. The HOA budget should adequately provide for the continual maintenance of the common elements.

LESSON 3 REVIEW QUESTIONS

1. If the subject is located in a(n) _____ market, then information on comparable properties will be plentiful.

2. To determine the value, similar properties that have transacted at a known sales price from the market are _____ to the subject.

3. The comparable properties are compared to the subject and the differences are accounted for in the sales grid as _____.

4. Adjustments are derived by performing a(n) _____.

5. If the comparable is _____ to the subject, the adjustment must be _____ to make the comparable similar to the subject.

6. If the sales price is $298,000 and the gross living area (GLA) is 2,000 square feet, $_____ would be entered as sales price/gross living area.

7. Appraiser's files, county recorder's records, MLSs, and lenders are all examples of _____ sources.

8. Seller financing with terms and conditions different from what is offered in the financing market is an examples of a special _____ or _____ concession.

9. A(n) _____ adjustment is the sum of all positive and negative adjustments.

10. A(n) _____ adjustment is the result of adding all of the adjustments for a comparable and ignoring the signs.

11. _____ takes place at the end of each approach to value and then at the end of the development phase of the appraisal process, but before reporting.

12. The _____ section is used for additional comments or explanations that do not fit within the various sections of the URAR.

13. The _____ approach is likely to be most applicable in newly constructed or relatively new properties.

14. There are two types of obsolescence: _____ and _____.

15. _____ obsolescence is a value loss as a result of the market's negative response to some functionality of the property.

16. _____ obsolescence is a value loss realized as a result of the market's negative response to something that is outside of the property lines.

17. The _____ approach to value has within it several methods of determining value based on the property's ability to create and maintain an income stream.

18. _____ are extracted from comparable sales in the market by dividing the value (sales price) by the monthly rent.

19. Multiplying the _____ extracted from the market by the monthly rent for the subject results in the indicated value using the income approach.

LESSON 3 REVIEW ANSWERS

1. active

2. compared

3. adjustments

4. paired sales analysis

5. superior; negative

6. 149

7. verification

8. sales; financing

9. net

10. gross

11. Reconciliation

12. additional comments

13. cost

14. functional; external

15. Functional

16. External

17. income

18. Gross income multipliers

19. GRM

LESSON 4: The URAR, Pages 4, 5, and 6

DEFINITIONS, ASSUMPTIONS AND LIMITING CONDITIONS, AND APPRAISER'S CERTIFICATION

According to Fannie Mae, the URAR is subject to the scope of work, intended use, intended user, definition of market value, statement of assumptions and limiting conditions, and certifications contained in the report form. Modifications, additions, or deletions to the intended use, intended user, definition of market value, and the statement of assumptions and limiting conditions are not permitted. The scope of work may be expanded to include any additional research or analysis necessary due to the complexity of the appraisal assignment. Fannie Mae further states that modifications or deletions to the certifications are also not permitted; however, additional certifications (added on a separate page) that do not alter the appraisal report are permitted. Additional certifications may include additional certifications required by state law, continuing education classes, or membership in appraisal organizations.

The appraiser must read and be familiar with pages 4, 5, and 6 of the URAR. Within these pages, the appraiser identifies the scope of work, intended use, and intended users; defines market value; and lists assumptions and limiting conditions and certifications indicating the appraiser's rule as being unbiased, impartial, and objective.

Appraiser   The appraiser signs the appraisal and completes the required information.

Supervisory Appraiser (only if required)   If there is a supervisory appraiser, he or she signs the report and completes the requested information. The supervisory appraiser also checks the appropriate boxes to indicate the extent of their role in the inspection of the subject and comparables. The supervisory appraiser agrees with the statements and conclusions and takes full responsibility for that agreement.

Uniform Residential Appraisal Report

File #

This report form is designed to report an appraisal of a one-unit property or a one-unit property with an accessory unit; including a unit in a planned unit development (PUD). This report form is not designed to report an appraisal of a manufactured home or a unit in a condominium or cooperative project.

This appraisal report is subject to the following scope of work, intended use, intended user, definition of market value, statement of assumptions and limiting conditions, and certifications. Modifications, additions, or deletions to the intended use, intended user, definition of market value, or assumptions and limiting conditions are not permitted. The appraiser may expand the scope of work to include any additional research or analysis necessary based on the complexity of this appraisal assignment. Modifications or deletions to the certifications are also not permitted. However, additional certifications that do not constitute material alterations to this appraisal report, such as those required by law or those related to the appraiser's continuing education or membership in an appraisal organization, are permitted.

SCOPE OF WORK: The scope of work for this appraisal is defined by the complexity of this appraisal assignment and the reporting requirements of this appraisal report form, including the following definition of market value, statement of assumptions and limiting conditions, and certifications. The appraiser must, at a minimum: (1) perform a complete visual inspection of the interior and exterior areas of the subject property, (2) inspect the neighborhood, (3) inspect each of the comparable sales from at least the street, (4) research, verify, and analyze data from reliable public and/or private sources, and (5) report his or her analysis, opinions, and conclusions in this appraisal report.

INTENDED USE: The intended use of this appraisal report is for the lender/client to evaluate the property that is the subject of this appraisal for a mortgage finance transaction.

INTENDED USER: The intended user of this appraisal report is the lender/client.

DEFINITION OF MARKET VALUE: The most probable price which a property should bring in a competitive and open market under all conditions requisite to a fair sale, the buyer and seller, each acting prudently, knowledgeably and assuming the price is not affected by undue stimulus. Implicit in this definition is the consummation of a sale as of a specified date and the passing of title from seller to buyer under conditions whereby: (1) buyer and seller are typically motivated; (2) both parties are well informed or well advised, and each acting in what he or she considers his or her own best interest; (3) a reasonable time is allowed for exposure in the open market; (4) payment is made in terms of cash in U. S. dollars or in terms of financial arrangements comparable thereto; and (5) the price represents the normal consideration for the property sold unaffected by special or creative financing or sales concessions* granted by anyone associated with the sale.

*Adjustments to the comparables must be made for special or creative financing or sales concessions. No adjustments are necessary for those costs which are normally paid by sellers as a result of tradition or law in a market area; these costs are readily identifiable since the seller pays these costs in virtually all sales transactions. Special or creative financing adjustments can be made to the comparable property by comparisons to financing terms offered by a third party institutional lender that is not already involved in the property or transaction. Any adjustment should not be calculated on a mechanical dollar for dollar cost of the financing or concession but the dollar amount of any adjustment should approximate the market's reaction to the financing or concessions based on the appraiser's judgment.

STATEMENT OF ASSUMPTIONS AND LIMITING CONDITIONS: The appraiser's certification in this report is subject to the following assumptions and limiting conditions:

1. The appraiser will not be responsible for matters of a legal nature that affect either the property being appraised or the title to it, except for information that he or she became aware of during the research involved in performing this appraisal. The appraiser assumes that the title is good and marketable and will not render any opinions about the title.

2. The appraiser has provided a sketch in this appraisal report to show the approximate dimensions of the improvements. The sketch is included only to assist the reader in visualizing the property and understanding the appraiser's determination of its size.

3. The appraiser has examined the available flood maps that are provided by the Federal Emergency Management Agency (or other data sources) and has noted in this appraisal report whether any portion of the subject site is located in an identified Special Flood Hazard Area. Because the appraiser is not a surveyor, he or she makes no guarantees, express or implied, regarding this determination.

4. The appraiser will not give testimony or appear in court because he or she made an appraisal of the property in question, unless specific arrangements to do so have been made beforehand, or as otherwise required by law.

5. The appraiser has noted in this appraisal report any adverse conditions (such as needed repairs, deterioration, the presence of hazardous wastes, toxic substances, etc.) observed during the inspection of the subject property or that he or she became aware of during the research involved in performing this appraisal. Unless otherwise stated in this appraisal report, the appraiser has no knowledge of any hidden or unapparent physical deficiencies or adverse conditions of the property (such as, but not limited to, needed repairs, deterioration, the presence of hazardous wastes, toxic substances, adverse environmental conditions, etc.) that would make the property less valuable, and has assumed that there are no such conditions and makes no guarantees or warranties, express or implied. The appraiser will not be responsible for any such conditions that do exist or for any engineering or testing that might be required to discover whether such conditions exist. Because the appraiser is not an expert in the field of environmental hazards, this appraisal report must not be considered as an environmental assessment of the property.

6. The appraiser has based his or her appraisal report and valuation conclusion for an appraisal that is subject to satisfactory completion, repairs, or alterations on the assumption that the completion, repairs, or alterations of the subject property will be performed in a professional manner.

Uniform Residential Appraisal Report   File

APPRAISER'S CERTIFICATION: The Appraiser certifies and agrees that:

1. I have, at a minimum, developed and reported this appraisal in accordance with the scope of work requirements stated in this appraisal report.

2. I performed a complete visual inspection of the interior and exterior areas of the subject property. I reported the condition of the improvements in factual, specific terms. I identified and reported the physical deficiencies that could affect the livability, soundness, or structural integrity of the property.

3. I performed this appraisal in accordance with the requirements of the Uniform Standards of Professional Appraisal Practice that were adopted and promulgated by the Appraisal Standards Board of The Appraisal Foundation and that were in place at the time this appraisal report was prepared.

4. I developed my opinion of the market value of the real property that is the subject of this report based on the sales comparison approach to value. I have adequate comparable market data to develop a reliable sales comparison approach for this appraisal assignment. I further certify that I considered the cost and income approaches to value but did not develop them, unless otherwise indicated in this report.

5. I researched, verified, analyzed, and reported on any current agreement for sale for the subject property, any offering for sale of the subject property in the twelve months prior to the effective date of this appraisal, and the prior sales of the subject property for a minimum of three years prior to the effective date of this appraisal, unless otherwise indicated in this report.

6. I researched, verified, analyzed, and reported on the prior sales of the comparable sales for a minimum of one year prior to the date of sale of the comparable sale, unless otherwise indicated in this report.

7. I selected and used comparable sales that are locationally, physically, and functionally the most similar to the subject property.

8. I have not used comparable sales that were the result of combining a land sale with the contract purchase price of a home that has been built or will be built on the land.

9. I have reported adjustments to the comparable sales that reflect the market's reaction to the differences between the subject property and the comparable sales.

10. I verified, from a disinterested source, all information in this report that was provided by parties who have a financial interest in the sale or financing of the subject property.

11. I have knowledge and experience in appraising this type of property in this market area.

12. I am aware of, and have access to, the necessary and appropriate public and private data sources, such as multiple listing services, tax assessment records, public land records and other such data sources for the area in which the property is located.

13. I obtained the information, estimates, and opinions furnished by other parties and expressed in this appraisal report from reliable sources that I believe to be true and correct.

14. I have taken into consideration the factors that have an impact on value with respect to the subject neighborhood, subject property, and the proximity of the subject property to adverse influences in the development of my opinion of market value. I have noted in this appraisal report any adverse conditions (such as, but not limited to, needed repairs, deterioration, the presence of hazardous wastes, toxic substances, adverse environmental conditions, etc.) observed during the inspection of the subject property or that I became aware of during the research involved in performing this appraisal. I have considered these adverse conditions in my analysis of the property value, and have reported on the effect of the conditions on the value and marketability of the subject property.

15. I have not knowingly withheld any significant information from this appraisal report and, to the best of my knowledge, all statements and information in this appraisal report are true and correct.

16. I stated in this appraisal report my own personal, unbiased, and professional analysis, opinions, and conclusions, which are subject only to the assumptions and limiting conditions in this appraisal report.

17. I have no present or prospective interest in the property that is the subject of this report, and I have no present or prospective personal interest or bias with respect to the participants in the transaction. I did not base, either partially or completely, my analysis and/or opinion of market value in this appraisal report on the race, color, religion, sex, age, marital status, handicap, familial status, or national origin of either the prospective owners or occupants of the subject property or of the present owners or occupants of the properties in the vicinity of the subject property or on any other basis prohibited by law.

18. My employment and/or compensation for performing this appraisal or any future or anticipated appraisals was not conditioned on any agreement or understanding, written or otherwise, that I would report (or present analysis supporting) a predetermined specific value, a predetermined minimum value, a range or direction in value, a value that favors the cause of any party, or the attainment of a specific result or occurrence of a specific subsequent event (such as approval of a pending mortgage loan application).

19. I personally prepared all conclusions and opinions about the real estate that were set forth in this appraisal report. If I relied on significant real property appraisal assistance from any individual or individuals in the performance of this appraisal or the preparation of this appraisal report, I have named such individual(s) and disclosed the specific tasks performed in this appraisal report. I certify that any individual so named is qualified to perform the tasks. I have not authorized anyone to make a change to any item in this appraisal report; therefore, any change made to this appraisal is unauthorized and I will take no responsibility for it.

20. I identified the lender/client in this appraisal report who is the individual, organization, or agent for the organization that ordered and will receive this appraisal report.

Uniform Residential Appraisal Report   File

21. The lender/client may disclose or distribute this appraisal report to: the borrower; another lender at the request of the borrower; the mortgagee or its successors and assigns; mortgage insurers; government sponsored enterprises; other secondary market participants; data collection or reporting services; professional appraisal organizations; any department, agency, or instrumentality of the United States; and any state, the District of Columbia, or other jurisdictions; without having to obtain the appraiser's or supervisory appraiser's (if applicable) consent. Such consent must be obtained before this appraisal report may be disclosed or distributed to any other party (including, but not limited to, the public through advertising, public relations, news, sales, or other media).

22. I am aware that any disclosure or distribution of this appraisal report by me or the lender/client may be subject to certain laws and regulations. Further, I am also subject to the provisions of the Uniform Standards of Professional Appraisal Practice that pertain to disclosure or distribution by me.

23. The borrower, another lender at the request of the borrower, the mortgagee or its successors and assigns, mortgage insurers, government sponsored enterprises, and other secondary market participants may rely on this appraisal report as part of any mortgage finance transaction that involves any one or more of these parties.

24. If this appraisal report was transmitted as an "electronic record" containing my "electronic signature," as those terms are defined in applicable federal and/or state laws (excluding audio and video recordings), or a facsimile transmission of this appraisal report containing a copy or representation of my signature, the appraisal report shall be as effective, enforceable and valid as if a paper version of this appraisal report were delivered containing my original hand written signature.

25. Any intentional or negligent misrepresentation(s) contained in this appraisal report may result in civil liability and/or criminal penalties including, but not limited to, fine or imprisonment or both under the provisions of Title 18, United States Code, Section 1001, et seq., or similar state laws.

SUPERVISORY APPRAISER'S CERTIFICATION: The Supervisory Appraiser certifies and agrees that:

1. I directly supervised the appraiser for this appraisal assignment, have read the appraisal report, and agree with the appraiser's analysis, opinions, statements, conclusions, and the appraiser's certification.

2. I accept full responsibility for the contents of this appraisal report including, but not limited to, the appraiser's analysis, opinions, statements, conclusions, and the appraiser's certification.

3. The appraiser identified in this appraisal report is either a sub-contractor or an employee of the supervisory appraiser (or the appraisal firm), is qualified to perform this appraisal, and is acceptable to perform this appraisal under the applicable state law.

4. This appraisal report complies with the Uniform Standards of Professional Appraisal Practice that were adopted and promulgated by the Appraisal Standards Board of The Appraisal Foundation and that were in place at the time this appraisal report was prepared.

5. If this appraisal report was transmitted as an "electronic record" containing my "electronic signature," as those terms are defined in applicable federal and/or state laws (excluding audio and video recordings), or a facsimile transmission of this appraisal report containing a copy or representation of my signature, the appraisal report shall be as effective, enforceable and valid as if a paper version of this appraisal report were delivered containing my original hand written signature.

APPRAISER

Signature_____
Name _____
Company Name _____
Company Address_____
_____
Telephone Number _____
Email Address_____
Date of Signature and Report_____
Effective Date of Appraisal _____
State Certification #_____
or State License # _____
or Other (describe) _____ State # _____
State _____
Expiration Date of Certification or License _____

ADDRESS OF PROPERTY APPRAISED

_____
_____

APPRAISED VALUE OF SUBJECT PROPERTY $ _____
LENDER/CLIENT
Name _____
Company Name _____
Company Address_____
_____
Email Address_____

SUPERVISORY APPRAISER (ONLY IF REQUIRED)

Signature _____
Name_____
Company Name _____
Company Address _____
_____
Telephone Number _____
Email Address _____
Date of Signature _____
State Certification #_____
or State License # _____
State _____
Expiration Date of Certification or License _____

SUBJECT PROPERTY

☐ Did not inspect subject property
☐ Did inspect exterior of subject property from street
   Date of Inspection _____
☐ Did inspect interior and exterior of subject property
   Date of Inspection _____

COMPARABLE SALES

☐ Did not inspect exterior of comparable sales from street
☐ Did inspect exterior of comparable sales from street
   Date of Inspection _____

LESSON 4 REVIEW QUESTIONS

True or False

1. Modifications, additions, or deletions to the intended use and intended user are not permitted.

2. Modifications, additions, or deletions to the definition of market value and the statement of assumptions are permitted.

3. Modifications, additions, or deletions to the limiting conditions are not permitted.

4. According to Fannie Mae, modifications or deletions to the certifications are permitted.

5. The scope of work may be expanded to include any additional research or analysis necessary due to the complexity of the appraisal assignment.

6. The supervisory appraiser agrees with the statements and conclusions but is not held responsible for the report content.

7. The supervisory appraiser checks the appropriate boxes to indicate the extent of their role in the inspection of the subject.

8. Appraisers are not permitted to add to the certifications.

9. Additional certifications may include additional certifications required by state law, continuing education classes, or membership in appraisal organizations.

10. Additional certifications must not alter the appraisal report.

LESSON 4 REVIEW ANSWERS

1. True

2. False

3. True

4. False

5. True

6. False

7. True

8. False

9. True

10. True

SECTION 3 REVIEW QUESTIONS

1. Residential appraisal report forms include Form 1025—Small Residential Income Property Appraisal, which is used to report an appraisal of a(n) _____-unit property.

2. Form 1007—Single-Family Comparable Rent Schedule is used to report market _____ for a conventional single-family investment property.

3. Form _____ is the required exhibit when the Form 1025—Small Residential Income Property Appraisal is used.

4. Form 1073—Individual Condominium Unit Appraisal Report is used to report an appraisal of a unit in a condominium project located within a(n) _____.

5. The first section on the URAR is the _____ section.

6. Currently, the URAR has ___ pages, not including required exhibits.

7. Fill out the blank improvements section of the URAR based on the following:

The subject, which was built in 1954, is a 1½-story Cape Cod home, with a full, unfinished, 1,005-square-foot basement that has a sump pump. After careful inspection, you determine that the home has an effective age of 30 years based on the overall condition of the property. The exterior finish of the home is part brick and part frame. The concrete foundation, the asphalt shingle roof, and the aluminum gutters are all in average condition. All of the windows of the home are single hung with storms and screen. The home does not have an attic and there is not an outside entrance for the basement, which does not show signs of dampness, settlement, or infestation.

Inside the home, the wooden floors and the carpeted areas are all in average condition. The drywall walls, wood trim, ceramic bathroom floor, and plastic bathroom wainscot are all in average condition. The home, which has a porch and a 2-car attached garage, is heated and cooled with gas-fueled, forced warm air and central air-conditioning. There is a 100-amp circuit breaker system and a 40-gallon hot water heater. The kitchen has a built-in refrigerator and range.

The above grade living area, which has 1,555 square feet, has a total of 6 rooms (living room, dining room, kitchen, 3 bedrooms, and 2 baths).

The subject, which is in average overall physical condition, is built with average quality construction typical for the area. No functional or external obsolescence is noted at the time of inspection and no physical deficiencies or adverse conditions were observed. The property conforms to the area.

General Description	Foundation	Exterior Description　materials/condition	Interior　materials/condition
Units ☐ One ☐ One with Accessory Unit	☐ Concrete Slab ☐ Crawl Space	Foundation Walls	Floors
# of Stories	☐ Full Basement ☐ Partial Basement	Exterior Walls	Walls
Type ☐ Det. ☐ Att. ☐ S-Det./End Unit	Basement Area　sq. ft.	Roof Surface	Trim/Finish
☐ Existing ☐ Proposed ☐ Under Const.	Basement Finish　%	Gutters & Downspouts	Bath Floor
Design (Style)	☐ Outside Entry/Exit ☐ Sump Pump	Window Type	Bath Wainscot
Year Built	Evidence of ☐ Infestation	Storm Sash/Insulated	Car Storage ☐ None
Effective Age (Yrs)	☐ Dampness ☐ Settlement	Screens	☐ Driveway　# of Cars
Attic ☐ None	Heating ☐ FWA ☐ HWBB ☐ Radiant	Amenities ☐ Woodstove(s) #	Driveway Surface
☐ Drop Stair ☐ Stairs	☐ Other　Fuel	☐ Fireplace(s) # ☐ Fence	☐ Garage　# of Cars
☐ Floor ☐ Scuttle	Cooling ☐ Central Air Conditioning	☐ Patio/Deck ☐ Porch	☐ Carport　# of Cars
☐ Finished ☐ Heated	☐ Individual ☐ Other	☐ Pool ☐ Other	☐ Att. ☐ Det. ☐ Built-in

Appliances ☐Refrigerator ☐Range/Oven ☐Dishwasher ☐Disposal ☐Microwave ☐Washer/Dryer ☐Other (describe)

Finished area **above** grade contains:　Rooms　Bedrooms　Bath(s)　Square Feet of Gross Living Area Above Grade

Additional features (special energy efficient items, etc.)

Describe the condition of the property (including needed repairs, deterioration, renovations, remodeling, etc.).

Are there any physical deficiencies or adverse conditions that affect the livability, soundness, or structural integrity of the property? ☐ Yes ☐ No If Yes, describe

Does the property generally conform to the neighborhood (functional utility, style, condition, use, construction, etc.)? ☐ Yes ☐ No If No, describe

(left margin vertical label: I M P R O V E M E N T S)

8. Fill out the blank contract section of the URAR based on the following:

You analyzed the sales contract for the subject dated March 2, 2007. The purchase price is listed as $265,000, and the seller is the current owner of public record. The contract did not indicate any special financial concessions.

I ☐ did ☐ did not analyze the contract for sale for the subject purchase transaction. Explain the results of the analysis of the contract for sale or why the analysis was not performed.

Contract Price $　Date of Contract　Is the property seller the owner of public record? ☐Yes ☐No Data Source(s)

Is there any financial assistance (loan charges, sale concessions, gift or downpayment assistance, etc.) to be paid by any party on behalf of the borrower? ☐ Yes ☐ No
If Yes, report the total dollar amount and describe the items to be paid.

(left margin vertical label: C O N T R A C T)

9. Fill out the blank site section of the URAR based on the following:

The subject's rectangular site has a residential view and is 30 feet wide and 125 feet long. The dimensions of the site and the shape are typical for the market area. The property is zoned RS-2, single-family residential district. After careful analysis, you determine that the property's current use is indeed the highest and best use of the property as improved.

The site has access to public utilities such as electricity, gas, water, and sewer. The asphalt street and paved alley are also public. After locating the subject property on a FEMA flood map, dated November 6, 2000, you find that the subject property, including the improvements, is not located in a flood zone (zone X). The flood map number is 17031C0515F. When you inspect the subject property and review the plat of survey, you do not find any adverse easements or encroachments.

Dimensions		Area	Shape	View			
Specific Zoning Classification		Zoning Description					
Zoning Compliance ☐ Legal ☐ Legal Nonconforming (Grandfathered Use) ☐ No Zoning ☐ Illegal (describe)							
Is the highest and best use of the subject property as improved (or as proposed per plans and specifications) the present use? ☐ Yes ☐ No If No, describe							
Utilities Public Other (describe)			Public Other (describe)		Off-site Improvements—Type	Public	Private
Electricity ☐ ☐		Water	☐ ☐		Street	☐	☐
Gas ☐ ☐		Sanitary Sewer	☐ ☐		Alley	☐	☐
FEMA Special Flood Hazard Area ☐ Yes ☐ No FEMA Flood Zone			FEMA Map #		FEMA Map Date		
Are the utilities and off-site improvements typical for the market area? ☐ Yes ☐ No If No, describe							
Are there any adverse site conditions or external factors (easements, encroachments, environmental conditions, land uses, etc.)? ☐ Yes ☐ No If Yes, describe							

OTHER RESIDENTIAL FORMS

Small Residential Income Property Appraisal Report   File

The purpose of this summary appraisal report is to provide the lender/client with an accurate, and adequately supported, opinion of the market value of the subject property.

SUBJECT

Property Address	City	State	Zip Code
Borrower	Owner of Public Record	County	
Legal Description			
Assessor's Parcel #	Tax Year	R.E. Taxes $	
Neighborhood Name	Map Reference	Census Tract	

Occupant ☐ Owner ☐ Tenant ☐ Vacant   Special Assessments $ ☐ PUD   HOA $ ☐ per year ☐ per month

Property Rights Appraised ☐ Fee Simple ☐ Leasehold ☐ Other (describe)

Assignment Type ☐ Purchase Transaction ☐ Refinance Transaction ☐ Other (describe)

Lender/Client   Address

Is the subject property currently offered for sale or has it been offered for sale in the twelve months prior to the effective date of this appraisal? ☐ Yes ☐ No

Report data source(s) used, offering price(s), and date(s).

CONTRACT

I ☐ did ☐ did not analyze the contract for sale for the subject purchase transaction. Explain the results of the analysis of the contract for sale or why the analysis was not performed.

Contract Price $ Date of Contract   Is the property seller the owner of public record? ☐Yes ☐No   Data Source(s)

Is there any financial assistance (loan charges, sale concessions, gift or downpayment assistance, etc.) to be paid by any party on behalf of the borrower? ☐ Yes ☐ No
If Yes, report the total dollar amount and describe the items to be paid.

NEIGHBORHOOD

Note: Race and the racial composition of the neighborhood are not appraisal factors.

Neighborhood Characteristics			2-4 Unit Housing Trends				2-4 Unit Housing		Present Land Use %	
Location ☐ Urban	☐ Suburban	☐ Rural	Property Values ☐ Increasing	☐ Stable	☐ Declining		PRICE	AGE	One-Unit	%
Built-Up ☐ Over 75%	☐ 25–75%	☐ Under 25%	Demand/Supply ☐ Shortage	☐ In Balance	☐ Over Supply		$ (000)	(yrs)	2-4 Unit	%
Growth ☐ Rapid	☐ Stable	☐ Slow	Marketing Time ☐ Under 3 mths	☐ 3–6 mths	☐ Over 6 mths		Low		Multi-Family	%
Neighborhood Boundaries							High		Commercial	%
							Pred.		Other	%

Neighborhood Description

Market Conditions (including support for the above conclusions)

SITE

Dimensions	Area	Shape	View

Specific Zoning Classification   Zoning Description

Zoning Compliance ☐ Legal ☐ Legal Nonconforming (Grandfathered Use) ☐ No Zoning ☐ Illegal (describe)

Is the highest and best use of the subject property as improved (or as proposed per plans and specifications) the present use? ☐ Yes ☐ No   If No, describe

Utilities	Public	Other (describe)		Public	Other (describe)	Off-site Improvements—Type	Public	Private
Electricity	☐	☐	Water	☐	☐	Street	☐	☐
Gas	☐	☐	Sanitary Sewer	☐	☐	Alley	☐	☐

FEMA Special Flood Hazard Area ☐ Yes ☐ No   FEMA Flood Zone   FEMA Map #   FEMA Map Date

Are the utilities and off-site improvements typical for the market area? ☐ Yes ☐ No   If No, describe

Are there any adverse site conditions or external factors (easements, encroachments, environmental conditions, land uses, etc.)? ☐ Yes ☐ No   If Yes, describe

IMPROVEMENTS

General Description			Foundation		Exterior Description	materials/condition	Interior	materials/condition
Units ☐ Two ☐ Three ☐ Four			☐ Concrete Slab ☐ Crawl Space		Foundation Walls		Floors	
☐ Accessory Unit (describe below)			☐ Full Basement ☐ Partial Basement		Exterior Walls		Walls	
# of Stories	# of bldgs.		Basement Area	sq. ft.	Roof Surface		Trim/Finish	
Type ☐ Det. ☐ Att. ☐ S-Det./End Unit			Basement Finish	%	Gutters & Downspouts		Bath Floor	
☐ Existing ☐ Proposed ☐ Under Const.			☐ Outside Entry/Exit ☐ Sump Pump		Window Type		Bath Wainscot	
Design (Style)			Evidence of ☐ Infestation		Storm Sash/Insulated		**Car Storage**	
Year Built			☐ Dampness ☐ Settlement		Screens		☐ None	
Effective Age (Yrs)			**Heating/Cooling**		**Amenities**		☐ Driveway # of Cars	
Attic ☐ None			☐ FWA ☐ HWBB ☐ Radiant		☐ Fireplace(s) # ☐ Woodstove(s) #		Driveway Surface	
☐ Drop Stair ☐ Stairs			☐ Other Fuel		☐ Patio/Deck ☐ Fence		☐ Garage # of Cars	
☐ Floor ☐ Scuttle			☐ Central Air Conditioning		☐ Pool ☐ Porch		☐ Carport # of Cars	
☐ Finished ☐ Heated			☐ Individual ☐ Other		☐ Other		☐ Att. ☐ Det. ☐ Built-in	

# of Appliances Refrigerator Range/Oven Dishwasher Disposal Microwave Washer/Dryer Other (describe)

Unit # 1 contains:	Rooms	Bedroom(s)	Bath(s)	Square feet of Gross Living Area
Unit # 2 contains:	Rooms	Bedroom(s)	Bath(s)	Square feet of Gross Living Area
Unit # 3 contains:	Rooms	Bedroom(s)	Bath(s)	Square feet of Gross Living Area
Unit # 4 contains:	Rooms	Bedroom(s)	Bath(s)	Square feet of Gross Living Area

Additional features (special energy efficient items, etc.)

Describe the condition of the property (including needed repairs, deterioration, renovations, remodeling, etc.).

Small Residential Income Property Appraisal Report   File

I M P R O V E M E N T S

Are there any physical deficiencies or adverse conditions that affect the livability, soundness, or structural integrity of the property? ☐ Yes ☐ No If Yes, describe

Does the property generally conform to the neighborhood (functional utility, style, condition, use, construction, etc.)? ☐ Yes ☐ No If No, describe

Is the property subject to rent control? ☐ Yes ☐ No If Yes, describe

C O M P A R A B L E R E N T A L D A T A

The following properties represent the most current, similar, and proximate comparable rental properties to the subject property. This analysis is intended to support the opinion of the market rent for the subject property.

FEATURE	SUBJECT	COMPARABLE RENTAL # 1	COMPARABLE RENTAL # 2	COMPARABLE RENTAL # 3
Address				
Proximity to Subject				
Current Monthly Rent	$	$	$	$
Rent/Gross Bldg. Area	$ sq. ft.	$ sq. ft.	$ sq. ft.	$ sq. ft.
Rent Control	☐ Yes ☐ No	☐ Yes ☐ No	☐ Yes ☐ No	☐ Yes ☐ No
Data Source(s)				
Date of Lease(s)				
Location				
Actual Age				
Condition				
Gross Building Area				

Unit Breakdown	Rm Count	Size Sq. Ft.	Rm Count	Size Sq. Ft.	Monthly Rent	Rm Count	Size Sq. Ft.	Monthly Rent	Rm Count	Size Sq. Ft.	Monthly Rent
	Tot Br Ba		Tot Br Ba			Tot Br Ba			Tot Br Ba		
Unit # 1					$			$			$
Unit # 2					$			$			$
Unit # 3					$			$			$
Unit # 4					$			$			$
Utilities Included											

Analysis of rental data and support for estimated market rents for the individual subject units reported below (including the adequacy of the comparables, rental concessions, etc.)

S U B J E C T R E N T S C H E D U L E

Rent Schedule: The appraiser must reconcile the applicable indicated monthly market rents to provide an opinion of the market rent for each unit in the subject property.

	Leases		Actual Rent			Opinion Of Market Rent		
	Lease Date		Per Unit		Total	Per Unit		Total
Unit #	Begin Date	End Date	Unfurnished	Furnished	Rent	Unfurnished	Furnished	Rent
1			$	$	$	$	$	$
2								
3								
4								

Comment on lease data		Total Actual Monthly Rent	$	Total Gross Monthly Rent	$
		Other Monthly Income (itemize)	$	Other Monthly Income (itemize)	$
		Total Actual Monthly Income	$	Total Estimated Monthly Income	$

Utilities included in estimated rents ☐ Electric ☐ Water ☐ Sewer ☐ Gas ☐ Oil ☐ Cable ☐ Trash collection ☐ Other (describe)

Comments on actual or estimated rents and other monthly income (including personal property)

P R I O R S A L E H I S T O R Y

I ☐ did ☐ did not research the sale or transfer history of the subject property and comparable sales. If not, explain

My research ☐ did ☐ did not reveal any prior sales or transfers of the subject property for the three years prior to the effective date of this appraisal.

Data source(s)

My research ☐ did ☐ did not reveal any prior sales or transfers of the comparable sales for the year prior to the date of sale of the comparable sale.

Data source(s)

Report the results of the research and analysis of the prior sale history of the subject property and comparable sales (report additional prior sales on page 4).

ITEM	SUBJECT	COMPARABLE SALE # 1	COMPARABLE SALE # 2	COMPARABLE SALE # 3
Date of Prior Sale/Transfer				
Price of Prior Sale/Transfer				
Data Source(s)				
Effective Date of Data Source(s)				

Analysis of prior sale history for the subject property and comparable sales

Small Residential Income Property Appraisal Report   File

There are	comparable properties currently offered for sale in the subject neighborhood ranging in price from $		to $	
There are	comparable sales in the subject neighborhood within the past twelve months ranging in sale price from $		to $	

FEATURE	SUBJECT	COMPARABLE SALE # 1		COMPARABLE SALE # 2		COMPARABLE SALE # 3	
Address							
Proximity to Subject							
Sale Price	$	$		$		$	
Sale Price/Gross Bldg. Area	$ sq. ft.	$ sq. ft.		$ sq. ft.		$ sq. ft.	
Gross Monthly Rent	$	$		$		$	
Gross Rent Multiplier							
Price Per Unit	$	$		$		$	
Price Per Room	$	$		$		$	
Price Per Bedroom	$	$		$		$	
Rent Control	☐ Yes ☐ No	☐ Yes ☐ No		☐ Yes ☐ No		☐ Yes ☐ No	
Data Source(s)							
Verification Source(s)							
VALUE ADJUSTMENTS	DESCRIPTION	DESCRIPTION	+ (-) Adjustment	DESCRIPTION	+ (-) Adjustment	DESCRIPTION	+ (-) Adjustment
Sale or Financing Concessions							
Date of Sale/Time							
Location							
Leasehold/Fee Simple							
Site							
View							
Design (Style)							
Quality of Construction							
Actual Age							
Condition							
Gross Building Area							
Unit Breakdown	Total Bedrooms Baths	Total Bdrms Baths		Total Bdrms Baths		Total Bdrms Baths	
Unit # 1							
Unit # 2							
Unit # 3							
Unit # 4							
Basement Description							
Basement Finished Rooms							
Functional Utility							
Heating/Cooling							
Energy Efficient Items							
Parking On/Off Site							
Porch/Patio/Deck							
Net Adjustment (Total)		☐ + ☐ -	$	☐ + ☐ -	$	☐ + ☐ -	$
Adjusted Sale Price		Net Adj. %		Net Adj. %		Net Adj. %	
of Comparables		Gross Adj. %	$	Gross Adj. %	$	Gross Adj. %	$
Adj. Price Per Unit (Adj. SP Comp / # of Comp Units)		$		$		$	
Adj. Price Per Room (Adj. SP Comp / # of Comp Rooms)		$		$		$	
Adj. Price Per Bedrm (Adj. SP Comp / # of Comp Bedrooms)		$		$		$	

Value Per Unit	$ X Units = $	Value Per GBA $ X GBA = $
Value Per Rm.	$ X Rooms = $	Value Per Bdrms. $ X Bdrms. = $

Summary of Sales Comparison Approach including reconciliation of the above indicators of value.

Indicated Value by Sales Comparison Approach $

Total gross monthly rent $ X gross rent multiplier (GRM)   = $ Indicated value by the Income Approach

Comments on income approach including reconciliation of the GRM

Indicated Value by: Sales Comparison Approach $ Income Approach $ Cost Approach (if developed) $

This appraisal is made ☐ "as is", ☐ subject to completion per plans and specifications on the basis of a hypothetical condition that the improvements have been completed, ☐ subject to the following repairs or alterations on the basis of a hypothetical condition that the repairs or alterations have been completed, or ☐ subject to the following required inspection based on the extraordinary assumption that the condition or deficiency does not require alteration or repair:

Based on a complete visual inspection of the interior and exterior areas of the subject property, defined scope of work, statement of assumptions and limiting conditions, and appraiser's certification, my (our) opinion of the market value, as defined, of the real property that is the subject of this report is $, as of   , which is the date of inspection and the effective date of this appraisal.

Small Residential Income Property Appraisal Report   File

ADDITIONAL COMMENTS

COST APPROACH TO VALUE (not required by Fannie Mae)

Provide adequate information for the lender/client to replicate the below cost figures and calculations.

Support for the opinion of site value (summary of comparable land sales or other methods for estimating site value)

ESTIMATED ☐ REPRODUCTION OR ☐ REPLACEMENT COST NEW	OPINION OF SITE VALUE... = $	
Source of cost data	Dwelling	Sq. Ft. @ $ ....=$
Quality rating from cost service Effective date of cost data		Sq. Ft. @ $ ....=$
Comments on Cost Approach (gross building area calculations, depreciation, etc.)	Garage/Carport	Sq. Ft. @ $ ....=$
	Total Estimate of Cost-New	....................= $
	Less Physical	Functional	External
	Depreciation	=$( )
	Depreciated Cost of Improvements......................................=$
	"As-is" Value of Site Improvements......................................=$
Estimated Remaining Economic Life (HUD and VA only) Years	Indicated Value By Cost Approach......................................=$

PROJECT INFORMATION FOR PUDs (if applicable)

Is the developer/builder in control of the Homeowners' Association (HOA)? ☐ Yes ☐ No   Unit type(s) ☐ Detached ☐ Attached

Provide the following information for PUDs ONLY if the developer/builder is in control of the HOA and the subject property is an attached dwelling unit.

Legal name of project

Total number of phases   Total number of units   Total number of units sold

Total number of units rented   Total number of units for sale   Data source(s)

Was the project created by the conversion of an existing building(s) into a PUD? ☐ Yes ☐ No   If Yes, date of conversion

Does the project contain any multi-dwelling units? ☐ Yes ☐ No Data source(s)

Are the units, common elements, and recreation facilities complete? ☐ Yes ☐ No If No, describe the status of completion.

Are the common elements leased to or by the Homeowners' Association? ☐ Yes ☐ No If Yes, describe the rental terms and options.

Describe common elements and recreational facilities.

Small Residential Income Property Appraisal Report   File

This report form is designed to report an appraisal of a two- to four-unit property, including a two- to four-unit property in a planned unit development (PUD). A two- to four-unit property located in either a condominium or cooperative project requires the appraiser to inspect the project and complete the project information section of the Individual Condominium Unit Appraisal Report or the Individual Cooperative Interest Appraisal Report and attach it as an addendum to this report.

This appraisal report is subject to the following scope of work, intended use, intended user, definition of market value, statement of assumptions and limiting conditions, and certifications. Modifications, additions, or deletions to the intended use, intended user, definition of market value, or assumptions and limiting conditions are not permitted. The appraiser may expand the scope of work to include any additional research or analysis necessary based on the complexity of this appraisal assignment. Modifications or deletions to the certifications are also not permitted. However, additional certifications that do not constitute material alterations to this appraisal report, such as those required by law or those related to the appraiser's continuing education or membership in an appraisal organization, are permitted.

SCOPE OF WORK: The scope of work for this appraisal is defined by the complexity of this appraisal assignment and the reporting requirements of this appraisal report form, including the following definition of market value, statement of assumptions and limiting conditions, and certifications. The appraiser must, at a minimum: (1) perform a complete visual inspection of the interior and exterior areas of the subject property, (2) inspect the neighborhood, (3) inspect each of the comparable sales from at least the street, (4) research, verify, and analyze data from reliable public and/or private sources, and (5) report his or her analysis, opinions, and conclusions in this appraisal report.

INTENDED USE: The intended use of this appraisal report is for the lender/client to evaluate the property that is the subject of this appraisal for a mortgage finance transaction.

INTENDED USER: The intended user of this appraisal report is the lender/client.

DEFINITION OF MARKET VALUE: The most probable price which a property should bring in a competitive and open market under all conditions requisite to a fair sale, the buyer and seller, each acting prudently, knowledgeably and assuming the price is not affected by undue stimulus. Implicit in this definition is the consummation of a sale as of a specified date and the passing of title from seller to buyer under conditions whereby: (1) buyer and seller are typically motivated; (2) both parties are well informed or well advised, and each acting in what he or she considers his or her own best interest; (3) a reasonable time is allowed for exposure in the open market; (4) payment is made in terms of cash in U. S. dollars or in terms of financial arrangements comparable thereto; and (5) the price represents the normal consideration for the property sold unaffected by special or creative financing or sales concessions* granted by anyone associated with the sale.

*Adjustments to the comparables must be made for special or creative financing or sales concessions. No adjustments are necessary for those costs which are normally paid by sellers as a result of tradition or law in a market area; these costs are readily identifiable since the seller pays these costs in virtually all sales transactions. Special or creative financing adjustments can be made to the comparable property by comparisons to financing terms offered by a third party institutional lender that is not already involved in the property or transaction. Any adjustment should not be calculated on a mechanical dollar for dollar cost of the financing or concession but the dollar amount of any adjustment should approximate the market's reaction to the financing or concessions based on the appraiser's judgment.

STATEMENT OF ASSUMPTIONS AND LIMITING CONDITIONS: The appraiser's certification in this report is subject to the following assumptions and limiting conditions:

1. The appraiser will not be responsible for matters of a legal nature that affect either the property being appraised or the title to it, except for information that he or she became aware of during the research involved in performing this appraisal. The appraiser assumes that the title is good and marketable and will not render any opinions about the title.

2. The appraiser has provided a sketch in this appraisal report to show the approximate dimensions of the improvements, including each of the units. The sketch is included only to assist the reader in visualizing the property and understanding the appraiser's determination of its size.

3. The appraiser has examined the available flood maps that are provided by the Federal Emergency Management Agency (or other data sources) and has noted in this appraisal report whether any portion of the subject site is located in an identified Special Flood Hazard Area. Because the appraiser is not a surveyor, he or she makes no guarantees, express or implied, regarding this determination.

4. The appraiser will not give testimony or appear in court because he or she made an appraisal of the property in question, unless specific arrangements to do so have been made beforehand, or as otherwise required by law.

5. The appraiser has noted in this appraisal report any adverse conditions (such as needed repairs, deterioration, the presence of hazardous wastes, toxic substances, etc.) observed during the inspection of the subject property or that he or she became aware of during the research involved in performing this appraisal. Unless otherwise stated in this appraisal report, the appraiser has no knowledge of any hidden or unapparent physical deficiencies or adverse conditions of the property (such as, but not limited to, needed repairs, deterioration, the presence of hazardous wastes, toxic substances, adverse environmental conditions, etc.) that would make the property less valuable, and has assumed that there are no such conditions and makes no guarantees or warranties, express or implied. The appraiser will not be responsible for any such conditions that do exist or for any engineering or testing that might be required to discover whether such conditions exist. Because the appraiser is not an expert in the field of environmental hazards, this appraisal report must not be considered as an environmental assessment of the property.

6. The appraiser has based his or her appraisal report and valuation conclusion for an appraisal that is subject to satisfactory completion, repairs, or alterations on the assumption that the completion, repairs, or alterations of the subject property will be performed in a professional manner.

Small Residential Income Property Appraisal Report   File

APPRAISER'S CERTIFICATION: The Appraiser certifies and agrees that:

1. I have, at a minimum, developed and reported this appraisal in accordance with the scope of work requirements stated in this appraisal report.

2. I performed a complete visual inspection of the interior and exterior areas of the subject property, including all units. I reported the condition of the improvements in factual, specific terms. I identified and reported the physical deficiencies that could affect the livability, soundness, or structural integrity of the property.

3. I performed this appraisal in accordance with the requirements of the Uniform Standards of Professional Appraisal Practice that were adopted and promulgated by the Appraisal Standards Board of The Appraisal Foundation and that were in place at the time this appraisal report was prepared.

4. I developed my opinion of the market value of the real property that is the subject of this report based on the sales comparison and income approaches to value. I have adequate market data to develop reliable sales comparison and income approaches to value for this appraisal assignment. I further certify that I considered the cost approach to value but did not develop it, unless otherwise indicated in this report.

5. I researched, verified, analyzed, and reported on any current agreement for sale for the subject property, any offering for sale of the subject property in the twelve months prior to the effective date of this appraisal, and the prior sales of the subject property for a minimum of three years prior to the effective date of this appraisal, unless otherwise indicated in this report.

6. I researched, verified, analyzed, and reported on the prior sales of the comparable sales for a minimum of one year prior to the date of sale of the comparable sale, unless otherwise indicated in this report.

7. I selected and used comparable sales that are locationally, physically, and functionally the most similar to the subject property.

8. I have not used comparable sales that were the result of combining a land sale with the contract purchase price of a home that has been built or will be built on the land.

9. I have reported adjustments to the comparable sales that reflect the market's reaction to the differences between the subject property and the comparable sales.

10. I verified, from a disinterested source, all information in this report that was provided by parties who have a financial interest in the sale or financing of the subject property.

11. I have knowledge and experience in appraising this type of property in this market area.

12. I am aware of, and have access to, the necessary and appropriate public and private data sources, such as multiple listing services, tax assessment records, public land records and other such data sources for the area in which the property is located.

13. I obtained the information, estimates, and opinions furnished by other parties and expressed in this appraisal report from reliable sources that I believe to be true and correct.

14. I have taken into consideration the factors that have an impact on value with respect to the subject neighborhood, subject property, and the proximity of the subject property to adverse influences in the development of my opinion of market value. I have noted in this appraisal report any adverse conditions (such as, but not limited to, needed repairs, deterioration, the presence of hazardous wastes, toxic substances, adverse environmental conditions, etc.) observed during the inspection of the subject property or that I became aware of during the research involved in performing this appraisal. I have considered these adverse conditions in my analysis of the property value, and have reported on the effect of the conditions on the value and marketability of the subject property.

15. I have not knowingly withheld any significant information from this appraisal report and, to the best of my knowledge, all statements and information in this appraisal report are true and correct.

16. I stated in this appraisal report my own personal, unbiased, and professional analysis, opinions, and conclusions, which are subject only to the assumptions and limiting conditions in this appraisal report.

17. I have no present or prospective interest in the property that is the subject of this report, and I have no present or prospective personal interest or bias with respect to the participants in the transaction. I did not base, either partially or completely, my analysis and/or opinion of market value in this appraisal report on the race, color, religion, sex, age, marital status, handicap, familial status, or national origin of either the prospective owners or occupants of the subject property or of the present owners or occupants of the properties in the vicinity of the subject property or on any other basis prohibited by law.

18. My employment and/or compensation for performing this appraisal or any future or anticipated appraisals was not conditioned on any agreement or understanding, written or otherwise, that I would report (or present analysis supporting) a predetermined specific value, a predetermined minimum value, a range or direction in value, a value that favors the cause of any party, or the attainment of a specific result or occurrence of a specific subsequent event (such as approval of a pending mortgage loan application).

19. I personally prepared all conclusions and opinions about the real estate that were set forth in this appraisal report. If I relied on significant real property appraisal assistance from any individual or individuals in the performance of this appraisal or the preparation of this appraisal report, I have named such individual(s) and disclosed the specific tasks performed in this appraisal report. I certify that any individual so named is qualified to perform the tasks. I have not authorized anyone to make a change to any item in this appraisal report; therefore, any change made to this appraisal is unauthorized and I will take no responsibility for it.

20. I identified the lender/client in this appraisal report who is the individual, organization, or agent for the organization that ordered and will receive this appraisal report.

Small Residential Income Property Appraisal Report   File

21. The lender/client may disclose or distribute this appraisal report to: the borrower; another lender at the request of the borrower; the mortgagee or its successors and assigns; mortgage insurers; government sponsored enterprises; other secondary market participants; data collection or reporting services; professional appraisal organizations; any department, agency, or instrumentality of the United States; and any state, the District of Columbia, or other jurisdictions; without having to obtain the appraiser's or supervisory appraiser's (if applicable) consent. Such consent must be obtained before this appraisal report may be disclosed or distributed to any other party (including, but not limited to, the public through advertising, public relations, news, sales, or other media).

22. I am aware that any disclosure or distribution of this appraisal report by me or the lender/client may be subject to certain laws and regulations. Further, I am also subject to the provisions of the Uniform Standards of Professional Appraisal Practice that pertain to disclosure or distribution by me.

23. The borrower, another lender at the request of the borrower, the mortgagee or its successors and assigns, mortgage insurers, government sponsored enterprises, and other secondary market participants may rely on this appraisal report as part of any mortgage finance transaction that involves any one or more of these parties.

24. If this appraisal report was transmitted as an "electronic record" containing my "electronic signature," as those terms are defined in applicable federal and/or state laws (excluding audio and video recordings), or a facsimile transmission of this appraisal report containing a copy or representation of my signature, the appraisal report shall be as effective, enforceable and valid as if a paper version of this appraisal report were delivered containing my original hand written signature.

25. Any intentional or negligent misrepresentation(s) contained in this appraisal report may result in civil liability and/or criminal penalties including, but not limited to, fine or imprisonment or both under the provisions of Title 18, United States Code, Section 1001, et seq., or similar state laws.

SUPERVISORY APPRAISER'S CERTIFICATION: The Supervisory Appraiser certifies and agrees that:

1. I directly supervised the appraiser for this appraisal assignment, have read the appraisal report, and agree with the appraiser's analysis, opinions, statements, conclusions, and the appraiser's certification.

2. I accept full responsibility for the contents of this appraisal report including, but not limited to, the appraiser's analysis, opinions, statements, conclusions, and the appraiser's certification.

3. The appraiser identified in this appraisal report is either a sub-contractor or an employee of the supervisory appraiser (or the appraisal firm), is qualified to perform this appraisal, and is acceptable to perform this appraisal under the applicable state law.

4. This appraisal report complies with the Uniform Standards of Professional Appraisal Practice that were adopted and promulgated by the Appraisal Standards Board of The Appraisal Foundation and that were in place at the time this appraisal report was prepared.

5. If this appraisal report was transmitted as an "electronic record" containing my "electronic signature," as those terms are defined in applicable federal and/or state laws (excluding audio and video recordings), or a facsimile transmission of this appraisal report containing a copy or representation of my signature, the appraisal report shall be as effective, enforceable and valid as if a paper version of this appraisal report were delivered containing my original hand written signature.

APPRAISER

Signature _____
Name _____
Company Name _____
Company Address _____

Telephone Number _____
Email Address _____
Date of Signature and Report _____
Effective Date of Appraisal _____
State Certification # _____
or State License # _____
or Other (describe)_____ State # _____
State _____
Expiration Date of Certification or License _____

ADDRESS OF PROPERTY APPRAISED

_____
_____

APPRAISED VALUE OF SUBJECT PROPERTY $ _____

LENDER/CLIENT
Name _____
Company Name _____
Company Address _____
_____
Email Address _____

SUPERVISORY APPRAISER (ONLY IF REQUIRED)

Signature _____
Name _____
Company Name _____
Company Address _____
_____
Telephone Number _____
Email Address _____
Date of Signature _____
State Certification # _____
or State License # _____
State _____
Expiration Date of Certification or License _____

SUBJECT PROPERTY

☐ Did not inspect subject property
☐ Did inspect exterior of subject property from street
　　Date of Inspection _____
☐ Did inspect interior and exterior of subject property
　　Date of Inspection _____

COMPARABLE SALES

☐ Did not inspect exterior of comparable sales from street
☐ Did inspect exterior of comparable sales from street
　　Date of Inspection _____

Operating Income Statement
One- to Four-Family Investment Property and Two- to Four-Family Owner-Occupied Property

Property Address

_____
Street   City   State   Zip Code

General Instructions: This form is to be prepared jointly by the loan applicant, the appraiser, and the lender's underwriter. The applicant must complete the following schedule indicating each unit's rental status, lease expiration date, current rent, market rent, and the responsibility for utility expenses. Rental figures must be based on the rent for an "unfurnished" unit.

	Currently Rented	Expiration Date	Current Rent Per Month	Market Rent Per Month	Utility Expense	Paid By Owner	Paid By Tenant
Unit No. 1	Yes ✓ No	_____	$_____	$_____	Electricity.............	☐	☐
Unit No. 2	Yes ☐ No ☐	_____	$_____	$_____	Gas....................	☐	☐
Unit No. 3	Yes ☐ No ☐	_____	$_____	$_____	Fuel Oil	☐	☐
Unit No. 4	Yes ☐ No ☐	_____	$_____	$_____	Fuel (Other)	☐	☐
Total			$ 0.00	$ 0.00	Water/Sewer	☐	☐
					Trash Removal	☐	☐

The applicant should complete all of the income and expense projections and for existing properties provide actual year-end operating statements for the past two years *(for new properties the applicant's projected income and expenses must be provided).* This Operating Income Statement and any previous operating statements the applicant provides must then be sent to the appraiser for review, comment, and/or adjustments next to the applicant's figures *(e.g., Applicant/Appraiser 288/300).* If the appraiser is retained to complete the form instead of the applicant, the lender must provide to the appraiser the aforementioned operating statements, mortgage insurance premium, HOA dues, leasehold payments, subordinate financing, and/or any other relevant information as to the income and expenses of the subject property received from the applicant to substantiate the projections. The underwriter should carefully review the applicant's/appraiser's projections and the appraiser's comments concerning those projections. The underwriter should make any final adjustments that are necessary to more accurately reflect any income or expense items that appear unreasonable for the market. *(Real estate taxes and insurance on these types of properties are included in PITI and not calculated as an annual expense item.)* Income should be based on current rents, but should not exceed market rents. When there are no current rents because the property is proposed, new, or currently vacant, market rents should be used.

Annual Income and Expense Projection for Next 12 months

Income *(Do not include income for owner-occupied units)*	By Applicant/Appraiser	Adjustments by Lender's Underwriter
Gross Annual Rental *(from unit(s) to be rented)*	$ _____	$ _____
Other Income *(include sources)*	+ _____	+ _____
Total	$ 0.00	$ 0.00
Less Vacancy/Rent Loss	− _____ (%)	− _____ (%)
Effective Gross Income	$ 0.00	$ 0.00

Expenses *(Do not include expenses for owner-occupied units)*

	By Applicant/Appraiser	Adjustments by Lender's Underwriter
Electricity	_____	_____
Gas	_____	_____
Fuel Oil	_____	_____
Fuel ....(Type - _____)	_____	_____
Water/Sewer	_____	_____
Trash Removal	_____	_____
Pest Control	_____	_____
Other Taxes or Licenses	_____	_____
Casual Labor	_____	_____
This includes the costs for public area cleaning, snow removal, etc., even though the applicant may not elect to contract for such services.		
Interior Paint/Decorating	_____	_____
This includes the costs of contract labor and materials that are required to maintain the interiors of the living units.		
General Repairs/Maintenance	_____	_____
This includes the costs of contract labor and materials that are required to maintain the public corridors, stairways, roofs, mechanical systems, grounds, etc.		
Management Expenses	_____	_____
These are the customary expenses that a professional management company would charge to manage the property.		
Supplies		
This includes the costs of items like light bulbs, janitorial supplies, etc.		
Total Replacement Reserves - See Schedule on Pg. 2..................	0.00	0.00
Miscellaneous	_____	_____
....	_____	_____
....	_____	_____
....	_____	_____
....	_____	_____
....	_____	_____
....	_____	_____
....	_____	_____
Total Operating Expenses	$ 0.00	$ 0.00

Freddie Mac
Form 998 Aug 88

This Form Must Be Reproduced By Seller
Page 1 of 2

Fannie Mae
Form 216 Aug 88

Replacement Reserve Schedule

Adequate replacement reserves must be calculated regardless of whether actual reserves are provided for on the owner's operating statements or are customary in the local market. This represents the total average yearly reserves. Generally, all equipment and components that have a remaining life of more than one year—such as refrigerators, stoves, clothes washers/dryers, trash compactors, furnaces, roofs, and carpeting, etc.—should be expensed on a replacement cost basis.

Equipment	Replacement Cost	Remaining Life		By Applicant/ Appraiser	Lender Adjustments
Stoves/Ranges .... @ $ _____ ea.	÷ ___ Yrs. x	_____ Units =$ _____	$ _____
Refrigerators .... @ $ _____ ea.	÷ ___ Yrs. x	_____ Units =$ _____	$ _____
Dishwashers .... @ $ _____ ea.	÷ ___ Yrs. x	_____ Units =$ _____	$ _____
A/C Units .... @ $ _____ ea.	÷ ___ Yrs. x	_____ Units =$ _____	$ _____
C. Washer/Dryers @ $ _____ ea.	÷ ___ Yrs. x	_____ Units =$ _____	$ _____
HW Heaters .... @ $ _____ ea.	÷ ___ Yrs. x	_____ Units =$ _____	$ _____
Furnace(s) .... @ $ _____ ea.	÷ ___ Yrs. x	_____ Units =$ _____	$ _____
(Other) .... @ $ _____ ea.	÷ ___ Yrs. x	_____ Units =$ _____	$ _____

Roof .... @ $ _____ ÷ ___ Yrs. x One Bldg. = $ _____ $ _____

Carpeting (Wall to Wall)   Remaining Life

(Units) _____ Total Sq. Yds. @ $____ Per Sq. Yd. ÷ ____Yrs. = $ _____ $ _____

(Public Areas) _____ Total Sq. Yds. @ $____ Per Sq. Yd. ÷ ____Yrs. = $ _____ $ _____

Total Replacement Reserves. (Enter on Pg. 1) $ 0.00 $ 0.00

Operating Income Reconciliation

$ _____ − $ _____ = $ 0.00 ÷ 12 = $ 0.00
Effective Gross Income   Total Operating Expenses   Operating Income   Monthly Operating Income

$ _____ − $ _____ = $ 0.00
Monthly Operating Income   Monthly Housing Expense   Net Cash Flow

(Note: Monthly Housing Expense includes principal and interest on the mortgage, hazard insurance premiums, real estate taxes, mortgage insurance premiums, HOA dues, leasehold payments, and subordinate financing payments.)

Underwriter's instructions for 2-4 Family Owner-Occupied Properties

- If Monthly Operating Income is a positive number, enter as "Net Rental Income" in the "Gross Monthly Income" section of Freddie Mac Form 65/Fannie Mae Form 1003. If Monthly Operating Income is a negative number, it must be included as a liability for qualification purposes.

- The borrower's monthly housing expense-to-income ratio must be calculated by comparing the total Monthly Housing Expense for the **subject property** to the borrower's stable monthly income.

Underwriter's instructions for 1-4 Family Investment Properties

- If Net Cash Flow is a positive number, enter as "Net Rental Income" in the "Gross Monthly Income" section of Freddie Mac Form 65/Fannie Mae Form 1003. If Net Cash Flow is a negative number, it must be included as a liability for qualification purposes.

- The borrower's monthly housing expense-to-income ratio must be calculated by comparing the total monthly housing expense for the borrower's **primary residence** to the borrower's stable monthly income.

Appraiser's Comments *(Including sources for data and rationale for the projections)*

_____   _____   _____
Appraiser Name   Appraiser Signature   Date

Underwriter's Comments and Rationale for Adjustments

_____   _____   _____
Underwriter Name   Underwriter Signature   Date

Individual Condominium Unit Appraisal Report   File

The purpose of this summary appraisal report is to provide the lender/client with an accurate, and adequately supported, opinion of the market value of the subject property.

S U B J E C T

Property Address		Unit #	City		State	Zip Code
Borrower		Owner of Public Record		County	
Legal Description					

Assessor's Parcel #   Tax Year   R.E. Taxes $

Project Name   Phase #   Map Reference   Census Tract

Occupant ☐ Owner ☐ Tenant ☐ Vacant   Special Assessments $ HOA $ ☐ per year ☐ per month

Property Rights Appraised ☐ Fee Simple ☐ Leasehold ☐ Other (describe)

Assignment Type ☐ Purchase Transaction ☐ Refinance Transaction ☐ Other (describe)

Lender/Client   Address

Is the subject property currently offered for sale or has it been offered for sale in the twelve months prior to the effective date of this appraisal? ☐ Yes ☐ No

Report data source(s) used, offering price(s), and date(s).

C O N T R A C T

I ☐ did ☐ did not analyze the contract for sale for the subject purchase transaction. Explain the results of the analysis of the contract for sale or why the analysis was not performed.

Contract Price $ Date of Contract   Is the property seller the owner of public record? ☐ Yes ☐ No Data Source(s)

Is there any financial assistance (loan charges, sale concessions, gift or downpayment assistance, etc.) to be paid by any party on behalf of the borrower? ☐ Yes ☐ No
If Yes, report the total dollar amount and describe the items to be paid.

N E I G H B O R H O O D

Note: Race and the racial composition of the neighborhood are not appraisal factors.

Neighborhood Characteristics			Condominium Unit Housing Trends			Condominium Housing		Present Land Use %	
Location ☐ Urban ☐ Suburban ☐ Rural			Property Values ☐ Increasing ☐ Stable ☐ Declining			PRICE	AGE	One-Unit	%
Built-Up ☐ Over 75% ☐ 25–75% ☐ Under 25%			Demand/Supply ☐ Shortage ☐ In Balance ☐ Over Supply			$ (000)	(yrs)	2-4 Unit	%
Growth ☐ Rapid ☐ Stable ☐ Slow			Marketing Time ☐ Under 3 mths ☐ 3–6 mths ☐ Over 6 mths			Low		Multi-Family	%
Neighborhood Boundaries						High		Commercial	%
						Pred.		Other	%

Neighborhood Description

Market Conditions (including support for the above conclusions)

P R O J E C T S I T E

Topography   Size   Density   View

Specific Zoning Classification   Zoning Description

Zoning Compliance ☐ Legal ☐ Legal Nonconforming – Do the zoning regulations permit rebuilding to current density? ☐ Yes ☐ No
☐ No Zoning ☐ Illegal (describe)

Is the highest and best use of the subject property as improved (or as proposed per plans and specifications) the present use? ☐ Yes ☐ No If No, describe

Utilities	Public	Other (describe)		Public	Other (describe)	Off-site Improvements—Type	Public	Private
Electricity	☐	☐	Water	☐	☐	Street	☐	☐
Gas	☐	☐	Sanitary Sewer	☐	☐	Alley	☐	☐

FEMA Special Flood Hazard Area ☐ Yes ☐ No FEMA Flood Zone   FEMA Map #   FEMA Map Date

Are the utilities and off-site improvements typical for the market area? ☐ Yes ☐ No If No, describe

Are there any adverse site conditions or external factors (easements, encroachments, environmental conditions, land uses, etc.)? ☐ Yes ☐ No If Yes, describe

P R O J E C T I N F O R M A T I O N

Data source(s) for project information

Project Description ☐ Detached ☐ Row or Townhouse ☐ Garden ☐ Mid-Rise ☐ High-Rise ☐ Other (describe)

General Description	General Description	Subject Phase		If Project Completed		If Project Incomplete	
# of Stories	Exterior Walls	# of Units		# of Phases		# of Planned Phases	
# of Elevators	Roof Surface	# of Units Completed		# of Units		# o f Planned Units	
☐ Existing ☐ Proposed	Total # Parking	# of Units For Sale		# of Units for Sale		# of Units for Sale	
☐ Under Construction	Ratio (spaces/units)	# of Units Sold		# of Units Sold		# of Units Sold	
Year Built	Type	# of Units Rented		# of Units Rented		# of Units Rented	
Effective Age	Guest Parking	# of Owner Occupied Units		# of Owner Occupied Units		# of Owner Occupied Units	

Project Primary Occupancy ☐ Principle Residence ☐ Second Home or Recreational ☐ Tenant

Is the developer/builder in control of the Homeowners' Association (HOA)? ☐ Yes ☐ No

Management Group – ☐ Homeowners' Association ☐ Developer ☐ Management Agent – Provide name of management company.

Does any single entity (the same individual, investor group, corporation, etc.) own more than 10% of the total units in the project? ☐ Yes ☐ No If Yes, describe

Was the project created by the conversion of an existing building(s) into a condominium? ☐ Yes ☐ No If Yes, describe the original use and the date of conversion.

Are the units, common elements, and recreation facilities complete (including any planned rehabilitation for a condominium conversion)? ☐ Yes ☐ No If No, describe

Is there any commercial space in the project? ☐ Yes ☐ No If Yes, describe and indicate the overall percentage of the commercial space.

Individual Condominium Unit Appraisal Report

File #

PROJECT INFORMATION

Describe the condition of the project and quality of construction.

Describe the common elements and recreational facilities.

Are any common elements leased to or by the Homeowners' Association? ☐ Yes ☐ No If Yes, describe the rental terms and options.

Is the project subject to ground rent? ☐ Yes ☐ No If Yes, $ _____ per year (describe terms and conditions)

Are the parking facilities adequate for the project size and type? ☐ Yes ☐ No If No, describe and comment on the effect on value and marketability.

PROJECT ANALYSIS

I ☐ did ☐ did not analyze the condominium project budget for the current year. Explain the results of the analysis of the budget (adequacy of fees, reserves, etc.), or why the analysis was not performed.

Are there any other fees (other than regular HOA charges) for the use of the project facilities? ☐ Yes ☐ No If Yes, report the charges and describe.

Compared to other competitive projects of similar quality and design, the subject unit charge appears ☐ High ☐ Average ☐ Low If High or Low, describe

Are there any special or unusual characteristics of the project (based on the condominium documents, HOA meetings, or other information) known to the appraiser? ☐ Yes ☐ No If Yes, describe and explain the effect on value and marketability.

Unit Charge $ _____ per month X 12 = $ _____ per year   Annual assessment charge per year per square feet of gross living area = $ _____

Utilities included in the unit monthly assessment ☐ None ☐ Heat ☐ Air Conditioning ☐ Electricity ☐ Gas ☐ Water ☐ Sewer ☐ Cable ☐ Other (describe)

UNIT DESCRIPTION

General Description	Interior materials/condition	Amenities	Appliances	Car Storage
Floor #	Floors	☐ Fireplace(s) #	☐ Refrigerator	☐ None
# of Levels	Walls	☐ Woodstove(s) #	☐ Range/Oven	☐ Garage ☐ Covered ☐ Open
Heating Type Fuel	Trim/Finish	☐ Deck/Patio	☐ Disp ☐ Microwave	# of Cars
☐ Central AC ☐ Individual AC	Bath Wainscot	☐ Porch/Balcony	☐ Dishwasher	☐ Assigned ☐ Owned
☐ Other (describe)	Doors	☐ Other	☐ Washer/Dryer	Parking Space #

Finished area **above** grade contains: _____ Rooms _____ Bedrooms _____ Bath(s) _____ Square Feet of Gross Living Area Above Grade

Are the heating and cooling for the individual units separately metered? ☐ Yes ☐ No If No, describe and comment on compatibility to other projects in the market area.

Additional features (special energy efficient items, etc.)

Describe the condition of the property (including needed repairs, deterioration, renovations, remodeling, etc.).

Are there any physical deficiencies or adverse conditions that affect the livability, soundness, or structural integrity of the property? ☐ Yes ☐ No If Yes, describe

Does the property generally conform to the neighborhood (functional utility, style, condition, use, construction, etc.)? ☐ Yes ☐ No If No, describe

PRIOR SALE HISTORY

I ☐ did ☐ did not research the sale or transfer history of the subject property and comparable sales. If not, explain

My research ☐ did ☐ did not reveal any prior sales or transfers of the subject property for the three years prior to the effective date of this appraisal.
Data source(s)

My research ☐ did ☐ did not reveal any prior sales or transfers of the comparable sales for the year prior to the date of sale of the comparable sale.
Data source(s)

Report the results of the research and analysis of the prior sale or transfer history of the subject property and comparable sales (report additional prior sales on page 3).

ITEM	SUBJECT	COMPARABLE SALE # 1	COMPARABLE SALE # 2	COMPARABLE SALE # 3
Date of Prior Sale/Transfer				
Price of Prior Sale/Transfer				
Data Source(s)				
Effective Date of Data Source(s)				

Analysis of prior sale or transfer history of the subject property and comparable sales.

Individual Condominium Unit Appraisal Report

File #

| There are | comparable properties currently offered for sale in the subject neighborhood ranging in price from $ | | to $ | |
| There are | comparable sales in the subject neighborhood within the past twelve months ranging in sale price from $ | | to $ | |

FEATURE	SUBJECT	COMPARABLE SALE # 1		COMPARABLE SALE # 2		COMPARABLE SALE # 3	
Address and Unit #							
Project Name and Phase							
Proximity to Subject							
Sale Price	$		$		$		$
Sale Price/Gross Liv. Area	$ sq. ft.	$ sq. ft.		$ sq. ft.		$ sq. ft.	
Data Source(s)							
Verification Source(s)							
VALUE ADJUSTMENTS	DESCRIPTION	DESCRIPTION	+(-) $ Adjustment	DESCRIPTION	+(-) $ Adjustment	DESCRIPTION	+(-) $ Adjustment
Sale or Financing Concessions							
Date of Sale/Time							
Location							
Leasehold/Fee Simple							
HOA Mo. Assessment							
Common Elements and Rec. Facilities							
Floor Location							
View							
Design (Style)							
Quality of Construction							
Actual Age							
Condition							
Above Grade Room Count	Total Bdrms. Baths	Total Bdrms. Baths		Total Bdrms. Baths		Total Bdrms. Baths	
Gross Living Area	sq. ft.	sq. ft.		sq. ft.		sq. ft.	
Basement & Finished Rooms Below Grade							
Functional Utility							
Heating/Cooling							
Energy Efficient Items							
Garage/Carport							
Porch/Patio/Deck							
Net Adjustment (Total)		☐ + ☐ -	$	☐ + ☐ -	$	☐ + ☐ -	$
Adjusted Sale Price of Comparables		Net Adj. % Gross Adj. %	$	Net Adj. % Gross Adj. %	$	Net Adj. % Gross Adj. %	$

(Left margin vertical label: SALES COMPARISON APPROACH)

Summary of Sales Comparison Approach

Indicated Value by Sales Comparison Approach $

INCOME APPROACH TO VALUE (not required by Fannie Mae)

(Left margin vertical label: INCOME)

Estimated Monthly Market Rent $ X Gross Rent Multiplier   = $ Indicated Value by Income Approach

Summary of Income Approach (including support for market rent and GRM)

Indicated Value by: Sales Comparison Approach $ Income Approach (if developed) $

(Left margin vertical label: RECONCILIATION)

This appraisal is made ☐ "as is", ☐ subject to completion per plans and specifications on the basis of a hypothetical condition that the improvements have been completed, ☐ subject to the following repairs or alterations on the basis of a hypothetical condition that the repairs or alterations have been completed, or ☐ subject to the following required inspection based on the extraordinary assumption that the condition or deficiency does not require alteration or repair:

Based on a complete visual inspection of the interior and exterior areas of the subject property, defined scope of work, statement of assumptions and limiting conditions, and appraiser's certification, my (our) opinion of the market value, as defined, of the real property that is the subject of this report is $, as of   , which is the date of inspection and the effective date of this appraisal.

Individual Condominium Unit Appraisal Report

This report form is designed to report an appraisal of a unit in a condominium project or a condominium unit in a planned unit development (PUD). This report form is not designed to report an appraisal of a manufactured home or a unit in a cooperative project.

This appraisal report is subject to the following scope of work, intended use, intended user, definition of market value, statement of assumptions and limiting conditions, and certifications. Modifications, additions, or deletions to the intended use, intended user, definition of market value, or assumptions and limiting conditions are not permitted. The appraiser may expand the scope of work to include any additional research or analysis necessary based on the complexity of this appraisal assignment. Modifications or deletions to the certifications are also not permitted. However, additional certifications that do not constitute material alterations to this appraisal report, such as those required by law or those related to the appraiser's continuing education or membership in an appraisal organization, are permitted.

SCOPE OF WORK: The scope of work for this appraisal is defined by the complexity of this appraisal assignment and the reporting requirements of this appraisal report form, including the following definition of market value, statement of assumptions and limiting conditions, and certifications. The appraiser must, at a minimum: (1) perform a complete visual inspection of the interior and exterior areas of the subject unit, (2) inspect and analyze the condominium project, (3) inspect the neighborhood, (4) inspect each of the comparable sales from at least the street, (5) research, verify, and analyze data from reliable public and/or private sources, and (6) report his or her analysis, opinions, and conclusions in this appraisal report.

INTENDED USE: The intended use of this appraisal report is for the lender/client to evaluate the property that is the subject of this appraisal for a mortgage finance transaction.

INTENDED USER: The intended user of this appraisal report is the lender/client.

MARKET VALUE: The most probable price which a property should bring in a competitive and open market under all conditions requisite to a fair sale, the buyer and seller, each acting prudently, knowledgeably and assuming the price is not affected by undue stimulus. Implicit in this definition is the consummation of a sale as of a specified date and the passing of title from seller to buyer under conditions whereby: (1) buyer and seller are typically motivated; (2) both parties are well informed or well advised, and each acting in what he or she considers his or her own best interest; (3) a reasonable time is allowed for exposure in the open market; (4) payment is made in terms of cash in U. S. dollars or in terms of financial arrangements comparable thereto; and (5) the price represents the normal consideration for the property sold unaffected by special or creative financing or sales concessions* granted by anyone associated with the sale.

*Adjustments to the comparables must be made for special or creative financing or sales concessions. No adjustments are necessary for those costs which are normally paid by sellers as a result of tradition or law in a market area; these costs are readily identifiable since the seller pays these costs in virtually all sales transactions. Special or creative financing adjustments can be made to the comparable property by comparisons to financing terms offered by a third party institutional lender that is not already involved in the property or transaction. Any adjustment should not be calculated on a mechanical dollar for dollar cost of the financing or concession but the dollar amount of any adjustment should approximate the market's reaction to the financing or concessions based on the appraiser's judgment.

STATEMENT OF ASSUMPTIONS AND LIMITING CONDITIONS: The appraiser's certification in this report is subject to the following assumptions and limiting conditions:

1. The appraiser will not be responsible for matters of a legal nature that affect either the property being appraised or the title to it, except for information that he or she became aware of during the research involved in performing this appraisal. The appraiser assumes that the title is good and marketable and will not render any opinions about the title.

2. The appraiser has provided a sketch in this appraisal report to show the approximate dimensions of the improvements. The sketch is included only to assist the reader in visualizing the property and understanding the appraiser's determination of its size.

3. The appraiser has examined the available flood maps that are provided by the Federal Emergency Management Agency (or other data sources) and has noted in this appraisal report whether any portion of the subject site is located in an identified Special Flood Hazard Area. Because the appraiser is not a surveyor, he or she makes no guarantees, express or implied, regarding this determination.

4. The appraiser will not give testimony or appear in court because he or she made an appraisal of the property in question, unless specific arrangements to do so have been made beforehand, or as otherwise required by law.

5. The appraiser has noted in this appraisal report any adverse conditions (such as needed repairs, deterioration, the presence of hazardous wastes, toxic substances, etc.) observed during the inspection of the subject property or that he or she became aware of during the research involved in performing this appraisal. Unless otherwise stated in this appraisal report, the appraiser has no knowledge of any hidden or unapparent physical deficiencies or adverse conditions of the property (such as, but not limited to, needed repairs, deterioration, the presence of hazardous wastes, toxic substances, adverse environmental conditions, etc.) that would make the property less valuable, and has assumed that there are no such conditions and makes no guarantees or warranties, express or implied. The appraiser will not be responsible for any such conditions that do exist or for any engineering or testing that might be required to discover whether such conditions exist. Because the appraiser is not an expert in the field of environmental hazards, this appraisal report must not be considered as an environmental assessment of the property.

6. The appraiser has based his or her appraisal report and valuation conclusion for an appraisal that is subject to satisfactory completion, repairs, or alterations on the assumption that the completion, repairs, or alterations of the subject property will be performed in a professional manner.

Individual Condominium Unit Appraisal Report

APPRAISER'S CERTIFICATION: The Appraiser certifies and agrees that:

1. I have, at a minimum, developed and reported this appraisal in accordance with the scope of work requirements stated in this appraisal report.

2. I performed a complete visual inspection of the interior and exterior areas of the subject property. I reported the condition of the improvements in factual, specific terms. I identified and reported the physical deficiencies that could affect the livability, soundness, or structural integrity of the property.

3. I performed this appraisal in accordance with the requirements of the Uniform Standards of Professional Appraisal Practice that were adopted and promulgated by the Appraisal Standards Board of The Appraisal Foundation and that were in place at the time this appraisal report was prepared.

4. I developed my opinion of the market value of the real property that is the subject of this report based on the sales comparison approach to value. I have adequate comparable market data to develop a reliable sales comparison approach for this appraisal assignment. I further certify that I considered the cost and income approaches to value but did not develop them, unless otherwise indicated in this report.

5. I researched, verified, analyzed, and reported on any current agreement for sale for the subject property, any offering for sale of the subject property in the twelve months prior to the effective date of this appraisal, and the prior sales of the subject property for a minimum of three years prior to the effective date of this appraisal, unless otherwise indicated in this report.

6. I researched, verified, analyzed, and reported on the prior sales of the comparable sales for a minimum of one year prior to the date of sale of the comparable sale, unless otherwise indicated in this report.

7. I selected and used comparable sales that are locationally, physically, and functionally the most similar to the subject property.

8. I have not used comparable sales that were the result of combining a land sale with the contract purchase price of a home that has been built or will be built on the land.

9. I have reported adjustments to the comparable sales that reflect the market's reaction to the differences between the subject property and the comparable sales.

10. I verified, from a disinterested source, all information in this report that was provided by parties who have a financial interest in the sale or financing of the subject property.

11. I have knowledge and experience in appraising this type of property in this market area.

12. I am aware of, and have access to, the necessary and appropriate public and private data sources, such as multiple listing services, tax assessment records, public land records and other such data sources for the area in which the property is located.

13. I obtained the information, estimates, and opinions furnished by other parties and expressed in this appraisal report from reliable sources that I believe to be true and correct.

14. I have taken into consideration the factors that have an impact on value with respect to the subject neighborhood, subject property, and the proximity of the subject property to adverse influences in the development of my opinion of market value. I have noted in this appraisal report any adverse conditions (such as, but not limited to, needed repairs, deterioration, the presence of hazardous wastes, toxic substances, adverse environmental conditions, etc.) observed during the inspection of the subject property or that I became aware of during the research involved in performing this appraisal. I have considered these adverse conditions in my analysis of the property value, and have reported on the effect of the conditions on the value and marketability of the subject property.

15. I have not knowingly withheld any significant information from this appraisal report and, to the best of my knowledge, all statements and information in this appraisal report are true and correct.

16. I stated in this appraisal report my own personal, unbiased, and professional analysis, opinions, and conclusions, which are subject only to the assumptions and limiting conditions in this appraisal report.

17. I have no present or prospective interest in the property that is the subject of this report, and I have no present or prospective personal interest or bias with respect to the participants in the transaction. I did not base, either partially or completely, my analysis and/or opinion of market value in this appraisal report on the race, color, religion, sex, age, marital status, handicap, familial status, or national origin of either the prospective owners or occupants of the subject property or of the present owners or occupants of the properties in the vicinity of the subject property or on any other basis prohibited by law.

18. My employment and/or compensation for performing this appraisal or any future or anticipated appraisals was not conditioned on any agreement or understanding, written or otherwise, that I would report (or present analysis supporting) a predetermined specific value, a predetermined minimum value, a range or direction in value, a value that favors the cause of any party, or the attainment of a specific result or occurrence of a specific subsequent event (such as approval of a pending mortgage loan application).

19. I personally prepared all conclusions and opinions about the real estate that were set forth in this appraisal report. If I relied on significant real property appraisal assistance from any individual or individuals in the performance of this appraisal or the preparation of this appraisal report, I have named such individual(s) and disclosed the specific tasks performed in this appraisal report. I certify that any individual so named is qualified to perform the tasks. I have not authorized anyone to make a change to any item in this appraisal report; therefore, any change made to this appraisal is unauthorized and I will take no responsibility for it.

20. I identified the lender/client in this appraisal report who is the individual, organization, or agent for the organization that ordered and will receive this appraisal report.

Individual Condominium Unit Appraisal Report   File

21. The lender/client may disclose or distribute this appraisal report to: the borrower; another lender at the request of the borrower; the mortgagee or its successors and assigns; mortgage insurers; government sponsored enterprises; other secondary market participants; data collection or reporting services; professional appraisal organizations; any department, agency, or instrumentality of the United States; and any state, the District of Columbia, or other jurisdictions; without having to obtain the appraiser's or supervisory appraiser's (if applicable) consent. Such consent must be obtained before this appraisal report may be disclosed or distributed to any other party (including, but not limited to, the public through advertising, public relations, news, sales, or other media).

22. I am aware that any disclosure or distribution of this appraisal report by me or the lender/client may be subject to certain laws and regulations. Further, I am also subject to the provisions of the Uniform Standards of Professional Appraisal Practice that pertain to disclosure or distribution by me.

23. The borrower, another lender at the request of the borrower, the mortgagee or its successors and assigns, mortgage insurers, government sponsored enterprises, and other secondary market participants may rely on this appraisal report as part of any mortgage finance transaction that involves any one or more of these parties.

24. If this appraisal report was transmitted as an "electronic record" containing my "electronic signature," as those terms are defined in applicable federal and/or state laws (excluding audio and video recordings), or a facsimile transmission of this appraisal report containing a copy or representation of my signature, the appraisal report shall be as effective, enforceable and valid as if a paper version of this appraisal report were delivered containing my original hand written signature.

25. Any intentional or negligent misrepresentation(s) contained in this appraisal report may result in civil liability and/or criminal penalties including, but not limited to, fine or imprisonment or both under the provisions of Title 18, United States Code, Section 1001, et seq., or similar state laws.

SUPERVISORY APPRAISER'S CERTIFICATION: The Supervisory Appraiser certifies and agrees that:

1. I directly supervised the appraiser for this appraisal assignment, have read the appraisal report, and agree with the appraiser's analysis, opinions, statements, conclusions, and the appraiser's certification.

2. I accept full responsibility for the contents of this appraisal report including, but not limited to, the appraiser's analysis, opinions, statements, conclusions, and the appraiser's certification.

3. The appraiser identified in this appraisal report is either a sub-contractor or an employee of the supervisory appraiser (or the appraisal firm), is qualified to perform this appraisal, and is acceptable to perform this appraisal under the applicable state law.

4. This appraisal report complies with the Uniform Standards of Professional Appraisal Practice that were adopted and promulgated by the Appraisal Standards Board of The Appraisal Foundation and that were in place at the time this appraisal report was prepared.

5. If this appraisal report was transmitted as an "electronic record" containing my "electronic signature," as those terms are defined in applicable federal and/or state laws (excluding audio and video recordings), or a facsimile transmission of this appraisal report containing a copy or representation of my signature, the appraisal report shall be as effective, enforceable and valid as if a paper version of this appraisal report were delivered containing my original hand written signature.

APPRAISER

Signature _____
Name _____
Company Name _____
Company Address _____
_____
Telephone Number _____
Email Address _____
Date of Signature and Report _____
Effective Date of Appraisal _____
State Certification # _____
or State License # _____
or Other _____ State # _____
State _____
Expiration Date of Certification or License _____

ADDRESS OF PROPERTY APPRAISED

_____
_____
APPRAISED VALUE OF SUBJECT PROPERTY $ _____
LENDER/CLIENT
Name _____
Company Name _____
Company Address _____
Email Address _____

SUPERVISORY APPRAISER (ONLY IF REQUIRED)

Signature _____
Name _____
Company Name _____
Company Address _____
_____
Telephone Number _____
Email Address _____
Date of Signature _____
State Certification # _____
or State License # _____
State _____
Expiration Date of Certification or License _____

SUBJECT PROPERTY
☐ Did not inspect subject property
☐ Did inspect exterior of subject property from street
    Date of Inspection _____
☐ Did inspect interior and exterior of subject property
    Date of Inspection _____

COMPARABLE SALES
☐ Did not inspect exterior of comparable sales from street
☐ Did inspect exterior of comparable sales from street
    Date of Inspection _____

SINGLE FAMILY COMPARABLE RENT SCHEDULE

This form is intended to provide the appraiser with a familiar format to estimate the market rent of the subject property. Adjustments should be made only for items of significant difference between the comparables and the subject property.

ITEM	SUBJECT	COMPARABLE NO. 1		COMPARABLE NO. 2		COMPARABLE NO. 3	
Address							
Proximity to Subject							
Date Lease Begins Date Lease Expires							
Monthly Rental	If Currently Rented: $	$		$		$	
Less: Utilities Furniture	$	$		$		$	
Adjusted Monthly Rent	$	$		$		$	
Data Source							
RENT ADJUSTMENTS	DESCRIPTION	DESCRIPTION	+(−) $ Adjustment	DESCRIPTION	+(−) $ Adjustment	DESCRIPTION	+(−) $ Adjustment
Rent Concessions							
Location/View							
Design and Appeal							
Age/Condition							
Above Grade Room Count	Total Bdrms Baths	Total Bdrms Baths		Total Bdrms Baths		Total Bdrms Baths	
Gross Living Area	Sq. Ft.	Sq. Ft.		Sq. Ft.		Sq. Ft.	
Other (e.g., basement, etc.)							
Other:							
Net Adj. (total)		☐ + ☐ − $		☐ + ☐ − $		☐ + ☐ − $	
Indicated Monthly Market Rent		$		$		$	

Comments on market data, including the range of rents for single family properties, an estimate of vacancy for single family rental properties, the general trend of rents and vacancy, and support for the above adjustments. (Rent concessions should be adjusted to the market, not to the subject property.)

Final Reconciliation of Market Rent:

I (WE) ESTIMATE THE MONTHLY MARKET RENT OF THE SUBJECT AS OF _____ TO BE $_____

Appraiser(s) SIGNATURE _____   Review Appraiser SIGNATURE _____
(If applicable)

NAME _____   NAME _____

This form must be reproduced by the Seller.

ANSWER KEY

SECTION 1 REVIEW ANSWERS

1. **c** identifying the problem.

2. **b** credible

3. **d** All of the above

4. **a** engagement

5. **c** client's

6. **c** Both a and b

7. **a** development; appraisal

8. **a** Critical

9. **a** incompetence.

10. **b** reasoning.

11. **b** Rhetoric

12. **c** Both a and b

13. **d** All of the above

14. **d** All of the above

15. **c** Education/qualifications, ethics/standards, and the public trust

16. **d** Both a and b

17. **c** my actions, actions of my peers, and the actions of the enforcement agencies of my profession.

18. **b** The Standard of Practice.

SECTION 2 REVIEW ANSWERS

1. **c** Both a and b

2. **b** audience

3. **d** All of the above

4. **d** All of the above

5. **c** Both a and b

6. **c** photos.

7. **c** famous quotes.

8. **d** All of the above

9. **a** always be avoided.

10. **b** Writing should be complicated. Long is better than short, complex is always better than simple.

11. **a** self-contained, summary, and restricted use.

12. **b** client

13. **b** signed

SECTION 3 REVIEW ANSWERS

1. 2–4

2. rent

3. 216

4. PUD

5. subject

6. 6

7.

General Description	Foundation	Exterior Description materials/condition	Interior materials/condition
Units ☒ One ☐ One with Accessory Unit	☐ Concrete Slab ☐ Crawl Space	Foundation Walls Concrete	Floors Wood/Carpet/Avg
# of Stories	☒ Full Basement ☐ Partial Basement	Exterior Walls Brick/Frame	Walls Drywall/Avg
Type ☒ Det. ☐ Att. ☐ S-Det./End Unit	Basement Area sq. ft.	Roof Surface Asphalt Shingle	Trim/Finish Wood/Avg
☒ Existing ☐ Proposed ☐ Under Const.	Basement Finish 0 %	Gutters & Downspouts Aluminum	Bath Floor Ceramic/Avg
Design (Style) Cape Cod	☐ Outside Entry/Exit ☒ Sump Pump	Window Type Single Hump	Bath Wainscot Plastic/Avg
Year Built 1954	Evidence of ☐ Infestation	Storm Sash/Insulated Yes	Car Storage ☐ None
Effective Age (Yrs) 30	☐ Dampness ☐ Settlement	Screens Yes	☐ Driveway # of Cars
Attic ☒ None	Heating ☒ FWA ☐ HWBB ☐ Radiant	Amenities ☐ Woodstove(s) #	Driveway Surface None
☐ Drop Stair ☐ Stairs	☐ Other Fuel	☐ Fireplace(s) # ☐ Fence	☒ Garage # of Cars 2
☐ Floor ☐ Scuttle	Cooling ☒ Central Air Conditioning	☐ Patio/Deck ☒ Porch	☐ Carport # of Cars
☐ Finished ☐ Heated	☐ Individual ☐ Other	☐ Pool ☐ Other	☐ Att. ☒ Det. ☐ Built-in

Appliances ☒Refrigerator ☒Range/Oven ☐Dishwasher ☐Disposal ☐Microwave ☐Washer/Dryer ☐Other (describe)

Finished area **above** grade contains: 6 Rooms 3 Bedrooms 2.0 Bath(s) 1,555 Square Feet of Gross Living Area Above Grade

Additional features (special energy efficient items, etc.) Gas forced air furnace; central air conditioning; 100 ampere circuit breaker electric; 40 gallon hot water heater; sump pump.

Describe the condition of the property (including needed repairs, deterioration, renovations, remodeling, etc.). The subject property is considered to be in average overall physical condition. The quality of construction is typical for the area. No functional or external obsolenscence was note at the time of inspection.

Are there any physical deficiencies or adverse conditions that affect the livability, soundness, or structural integrity of the property? ☐ Yes ☒ No If Yes, describe

Does the property generally conform to the neighborhood (functional utility, style, condition, use, construction, etc.)? ☒ Yes ☐ No If No, describe

8.

I ☒ did ☐ did not analyze the contract for sale for the subject purchase transaction. Explain the results of the analysis of the contract for sale or why the analysis was not performed. The subject is under a contract of sale with a purchase price of $265,000 as of 03/02/07

Contract Price $ 265,000 Date of Contract 03/02/07 Is the property seller the owner of public record? ☒Yes ☐No Data Source(s) Public Record

Is there any financial assistance (loan charges, sale concessions, gift or downpayment assistance, etc.) to be paid by any party on behalf of the borrower? ☐ Yes ☒ No
If Yes, report the total dollar amount and describe the items to be paid. N/A No financing concessions were reported in the contract

9.

Dimensions 30 x 125 Area 3,750 Sq. Ft. Shape Rectangular View Residential

Specific Zoning Classification RS-2 Zoning Description Single Family Residential District

Zoning Compliance ☒ Legal ☐ Legal Nonconforming (Grandfathered Use) ☐ No Zoning ☐ Illegal (describe)

Is the highest and best use of the subject property as improved (or as proposed per plans and specifications) the present use? ☒ Yes ☐ No If No, describe

Utilities	Public	Other (describe)		Public	Other (describe)	Off-site Improvements—Type	Public	Private
Electricity	☒	☐	Water	☒	☐	Street	☒	☐
Gas	☒	☐	Sanitary Sewer	☒	☐	Alley	☒	☐

FEMA Special Flood Hazard Area ☐ Yes ☒ No FEMA Flood Zone X FEMA Map # 17031C0515F FEMA Map Date 11/6/2000

Are the utilities and off-site improvements typical for the market area? ☒ Yes ☐ No If No, describe

Are there any adverse site conditions or external factors (easements, encroachments, environmental conditions, land uses, etc.)? ☐ Yes ☒ No If Yes, describe

The size and shape of this site is typical of most sites within this neighborhood. There are no apparent adverse easements or encroachments. The subject property is located in a FEMA Zone X location.

INDEX